D0453228

Contents

To Daniel W. Hardy

Transforming Church

Robin Greenwood is a practical theologian with over 30 years' experience of reflecting strategically on the character and task of the Church. He has resourced conferences and workshops in several provinces of the Anglican Communion and written widely on ministry issues. Currently he is Ministry Officer for the Church in Wales and a director of the Edward King Institute for Ministry Development. He is a member of the Third Order of the Society of St Francis. Robin is married and has three adult children.

Foreword

What are the temptations for the Christian Church today? Well, we might say that complacency, which would once have been such a temptation, is unlikely to look like a plausible option now. But there is more than one kind of complacency, of course, including the complacent assurance that you have identified a problem than can now be clearly addressed for the first time. There is the complacent conviction that, while the Church is indeed in a mess, it is quite clear whose fault it is (liberals, conservatives, laity, vicars, bishops, new hymns, old hymns, reformed liturgy, unreformed liturgy . . .); and that odd sort of satisfaction that comes from accepting and 'naturalizing' the response of depression and powerlessness, based on the certainty that the decisions that matter are always being taken somewhere else.

I think that Robin Greenwood's book is a sustained assault on these and related kinds of complacency. As he acknowledges more than once, this means that he is not proposing a panacea for the supposed ills of the Christian Church; his aim is to shift us from both passivity and glib problem-solving to an honest examination of why the reality of the Church matters at all. He is clear that most would-be global solutions are at best patronizing, at worst schemes that just reinforce unreality. And he is also clear that it is only as a whole group of people who call themselves Christian come to own and give voice to a shared sense of what, as Church, they most deeply want that anything like renewal will come.

If there is a core difficulty in the way we understand Church – granted all the dangers of trying to say anything like this – perhaps it is that we aren't used to asking about what we want. Not what we want *of* the Church: that just takes us into the consumerist mindset; but what we want *as* the Church, what this community seeks to be and do. The more we see it as essentially there to meet a cluster of not too coherent needs, the less it can be a community of intentions and purposes. But if it is not in some intelligible way such a community, it deserves the fate that currently seems not unlikely, of being submerged in a competitive market of institutions that meet needs.

So we don't need things made more simple, necessarily; we need things made deeper, more patient, more conversational, and we need therefore a style of educating and animating communities that more adequately models what we believe about the act and nature of God. What Robin Greenwood offers us here is a carefully woven reflection on how to move into this theological seriousness, characterized by an impressive flexibility as to how that is to be realized in diverse contexts, and sympathetically illustrated by some worked examples. It is important that these are so different; they leave space for the reader. That might indeed be said of the book as a whole. It manages to be profoundly timely without being fashionable, and to direct us to primary questions. It should be very welcome.

Rowan Williams

Acknowledgements

Much of the reflection leading to this book took place among colleagues in the Diocese of Chelmsford in a time of uncertainty and pain about the future shape of ministries and resources for education and training. Among them I acknowledge especially the diocesan Local Ministry Group and the West Ham Archdeaconry Local Ministry Group. In particular I wish to record my appreciation of the warm comradeship of Laura Garnham, Roger Matthews and Philip Ritchie who continue to carry responsibility for encouraging the flourishing of local ministry. Recently having taken up the role as Officer for Ministry in the Church in Wales, I am grateful for the stimulus of Robert Patterson and Provincial Team members as well as to new colleagues and friends in many forms of ministry throughout Wales.

Throughout the past five years during which this book has been written a constant dialogue partner has been my wife Claire. Her own explorations into the theory and practice of Gestalt psychotherapy have given me opportunities to stretch my theology, imagination and living, especially through contact with field theories. I am grateful for this love and friendship that strengthen my willingness and ability to recognize God's presence and direction in ways I had not thought of before. I acknowledge too how, in their different ways, our children Peter, Tim and Katherine have challenged and supported this work.

One of the privileges of recent years has been to act as Co-director for the Edward King Institute for Ministry Development, which produces the journal *Ministry* and, as a critical friend to the Church, every second year hosts a national consultation on a significant area of debate and experiment. In recent years sharing in common tasks with EKI colleagues has offered a particular support, professionally and personally. Especially I want to offer warm thanks to Christopher Laurence, Caroline Pascoe, Janice Price and Trevor Wilmott. Over the past two years I have shared with a small team the task of drafting the Church of England's current policy document on Continuing Ministerial Education. All of that has inevitably nourished my thinking. I wish to thank all the members and especially Margaret Jackson who acted as secretary.

I want to acknowledge a debt of gratitude for the personal support and creative stimulation of other ministry developers internationally. Among these I mention the national network of Ministry Development Officers and also Ray Armstead, Robin Briggs, Tony Chesterman, Shirley Cutbush, Robert Daborn, Jenny Dawson, Barrie Guage, Peter Harding, Cilla Hawkes, Richard Impey, Jim Kelsey, Ann McElligot, Julia Mourant, John Noble, Gordon Oliver, Alister Palmer, Donald Pickard, Christopher Race, Peter Sedgwick, Trevor Smith, John Suddards, Hazel Whitehead, Robert Wiggs and Clyde Wood. And to this list I add my gratitude for the many conversations with Stephen Brown, Alan Payne and Malcolm Squires.

I continue to be indebted to Daniel W. Hardy whose regular and patient listening, encouragement and sharing his own passion for the greater competence of the Church has contributed to the growth in my theological thinking and confidence in attempting to see how differing disciplines interact.

While taking final responsibility for the accuracy of this text, I am grateful to John Polkinghorne for his advice on the section containing material associated with physics. I am grateful, too, to the editor of *Crucible* for permission to reproduce material from my article, 'Mission, Community and the Local Church', July 2001, pp. 155–67, in Chapter 3. Among those who practise psychotherapy I wish to acknowledge many rich exchanges with Maggie McKenzie, Felicity Moore, Anthony Stone and Henry Wilson. I also wish to thank Liz Marsh at SPCK for her steady support and encouragement. Finally, without the exemplary secretarial assistance of both Ros Giddings and Jenny Johnson, other matters of administration would have greatly slowed down the final production of this book.

Introduction

My own awareness of being changed, often unwillingly, through the transforming power of Jesus Christ has mostly been in communities aiming to be distinguished by worship carefully prepared and joyfully enacted by everyone, by mutual care, thoughtful reflection, silent prayer, concern for those in need, a radical openness to all, and a corporate energy for demonstrating and interpreting faith to others. For example, I recall with thankfulness the rural Yorkshire parish church and primary school where I first learned of God's protecting and demanding love; the university and theological college communities that taught me to pray, to value the contribution of every person, and to think; the parishes and cathedrals in which I worked with others to expect so much of God and of one another in communal relations; and the family where I have learned to confront so many of my resistances to being loved and to relating to others through feeling as well as thought. I give thanks also for so many temporary communities and teams, small and large in the itinerant life of a ministry developer – and for the encouragement of Franciscan communities and others committed daily to growing in openness to God and to the whole of creation. Finally my thanks are for the swelling numbers of ministry teams which in their particular contexts are learning to be a catalyst and focus for the engagement of many with God's life in the entire world.

God as shown to us in Jesus is decisively encountered in worshipping communities. As exemplifications of Christian belief, face-to-face Christian communities, in giving direction, purpose and joy to participants, offer to the world a witness of what life can be. Of course this positive account of the Church's vocation needs to be tempered by the reality we encounter in which those of different or of no faith so often are a challenge to the Church in their own clear-sightedness about 'God's Kingdom'. After more than 30 years as an Anglican priest my sense is that the Church, though often harassed, battered and uncertain, has much to offer to life in society now. This is neither through being cut off from the rest of society nor through a preoccupation with defining 'necessary' beliefs and ethical stances. Rather the Church's vocation is to be explored in communities that echo Jesus' own delight and preoccupation with being together in ways that praise God and show, through a multiplicity of practicalities and the imaginative use of symbols, how God relates to the whole creation. The four Gospel writers reveal that our personal relationship with God and the final fruition of all creation cannot rightly be separated. A key aspect of my present inquiry hinges on the fact that in theory and practice the Church's ability to communicate with integrity cannot be detached from its everyday way of conducting itself.

Whether we like it or not, the Church's life, created and expressed in the entire celebration of the Eucharist and in the complementary ministries of all the baptized members of the worshipping community, is a practical embodiment or an open book of its beliefs in the world. Paul described the local church as a letter of recommendation 'written on our hearts, to be known and read by all ... a letter of Christ ... written not with ink but with the Spirit of the living God ... on tablets of human hearts' (see 2 Cor. 3.1–3). So often it has been the experience of the public that the performance of local churches is disappointing, unambitious and uncompelling. Thankfully the Church, as a sign of who God is, is supported by Christ and the Spirit to be a means of grace, the mediation of God's life in the world and a foretaste of God's Kingdom (see De Lubac, 1949; ARCIC, 1982). Our commission requires us continually to be reconceiving how, in its local and diocesan forms, as diverse communities facing God, one another and the whole world, the Church can better demonstrate and reinforce its relevance to people of today in Britain. There are powerful forces in competition with 'belonging' to societies and organizations today. The whole notion of being committed to complex and demanding institutions is suspected by the under-thirties age group and is clearly being replaced by fragmentary, temporary and electronic networks. Further, church attendance has to compete with forms of spiritual enquiry and practice that make no credal or institutional demands. At the level of sheer attractiveness, Church is in the market with Sky TV, family shopping, sport, and garden 'makeovers'. However, I believe it is possible and necessary to look with confidence to reconfiguring ourselves as Church today to continue to serve God's will through local community living, available to all in every part of the country. This book is a contribution to the process of the present reconsideration of how this is might be conceivable, affordable, achievable, educated, led and developed.

Transforming Church does not intend to promote a naive view that the Church requires no leadership. Rather my project in this book is to invite traditional (or as some would call it 'proper') church life to learn more about dynamic, continuing, interactive processes of re-visioning and supporting thought and practice about the character and work of the Church (ecclesiology). We could spend energy exploring the roots of the term 'hierarchy' and even pronounce it benign but misunderstood. But sometimes words that have been dominant over a long period are simply due for a rest because they carry an overlay of unwanted messages. Although most of our personal experiences of those in church 'hierarchy' today are friendly rather than harmful, a concern with primacy, rank, and the honour and dignity of superior office jars considerably with new insights into the nature of the Church.

Inherited understandings of the nature of the Church and its ministry are currently in flux as assumptions built on previously persuasive models are rapidly losing credibility. Anglicans are challenged now from one side by the lively worship and cellular community living of some of the younger Churches and on the other by the steady withdrawal of the public at large from institutional religion. Those who attempt to instigate change or refuse to support inherited assumptions are often punished or left in the cold by those who experience profound discomfort in the face of alternative possibilities for how all Christians equally participate in God's work in the world. The particular authority and form of ordained ministry on whom everything has rested for so long is now inevitably a particular focus of church debate and practical experiment in the light of recent decades of exploring the summons of everyone to ministry on account of their belonging to the eucharistic community.

My particular window-on-reality has recently been as a joint-leader and member of a team of educational and training specialists, consulting with church councils and ministry teams, addressing dioceses and provinces, taking part in informal conversations, debating with research students, leading retreats, preaching at ordinations, belonging to the Franciscan Third Order, co-directing the Edward King Institute for Ministry Development (EKI), jointly leading national consultations on ministry, co-ordinating the national network of Ministry Development Officers, chairing the Continuing Ministerial and Development Panel of the Ministry Division of the Archbishops' Council (Church of England), and acting as theological reflector to an international consultation in San Francisco on 'total ministry'. In the midst of the institutional Church's present limitations and distortions, the questions we have wrestled with in such gatherings include: 'God – who are you?', 'Who are we?', 'Why Church?', 'What do we mean when we say "Church"?', 'For how long will or should our particular way of being Church survive?', 'What kind of Church is God wanting here and now?', 'How do we make responsible, participative decisions on the structures of authority and distribution of power in the Church?', 'What is our responsibility?', 'How shall we bring about desired change?' and 'How shall we measure achievement?'

The conclusion of a five-year period as a diocesan Ministry Development Officer is a good time for reflecting on current experiments and new patterns of language about mission and ministry in the local church.

So I begin this book with a process of taking stock, writing specifically from within the Anglican Church in Britain, but believing that the preoccupations, shortcomings and strategies explored here are shared by many long-standing Churches worldwide. I offer my immediate and concrete impressions in the spirit of a critical friend for whom membership of the Church, however often uncomfortable, remains a valued and safe mainstay of my human and spiritual development.

My approach in the first chapter is to reflect on where we allow energy to flow and where we inhibit or block it. If we can be more clear and honest about this it should make room for further thought on ways of conceiving and furthering a wide and rich dynamic of engagement between God, churches, communities and people. At a time when the viability of public Christian life is uncertain, increasingly financially vulnerable, with consequent pressure for those whose chief way of earning their living is in professional church employment, I argue that we shall need a combination of determination, tenacity, passionate caring, deep thought, prayer and worship to discover how as *Church* to co-operate differently with the triune God.

I am certainly not about to fill these pages with a complaining diatribe on the organizational conflicts, dilemmas and uncertainties of the Church, as if I am not a participant or part of the problem. However, I need to anchor this study in an opening report on what are the real matters currently facing us. My own reading of the situation in Britain is that we are living through a period when the Church and its public ministers – experiencing a loss of clear identity, public relevance and viable self-understanding – are faced with the urgent need for tough thinking and deepening spiritual discipline in order to counter the rush to polarized and simplistic solutions. I believe this is compounded by two aspects of the same reality.

At the individual level, despite immense commitment to practical ministry, it is my belief that a very large proportion of serving clergy, Readers and accredited laity are not giving sufficient time to examining or even acknowledging the deeply rooted assumptions behind their practice, which were probably the dominant and effective ones at the time of their initial training. Second there is a marked absence in dioceses of reliable, workable processes for arriving at coherent and agreed visions and strategies. An accurate picture of the situation is difficult to obtain. This is partly because of a general unwillingness to recognize what is really happening or to reflect seriously on why problems of decision-making or frustrations in communication have arisen, in order, if possible, to avoid repeating them.

Here is one creative example of what can develop when we face up to the fact that many local church leaders face truly desperate problems – not necessarily of their own making, but as the sharp end of institutional difficulties. A recent experiment in clergy 'support groups' (funded by bishops and led by a psychotherapist with experience of group facilitation) shows in general terms that the sharp issues include:

- a sense of isolation among clergy;
- anxiety about a changing role and job security;
- clergy chapters that do not offer nourishment;
- a lack of value and care from the diocese or parish;
- receiving blame for not shielding congregations from a sense of loss, fear or disintegration;
- lack of knowledge of where to ask for support;
- the management of time off;
- dealing with hurts inflicted through working in a church environment;
- deciding whether to stay or move on;
- finding resources to grow in ability to do the job; and
- the dilemmas of the rapidly growing number of clergy married couples.

Despite some initial resistance, the deliberate offering by a diocese of a safe place to explore such issues allowed for both honesty and attention to seeing what changes could be supported. One of the underlying themes of this book is asking what bishops and others can contribute from their particular leadership roles to reshape the Church. What do they in particular need to contribute to our moving away from outworn models and to create optimal conditions for the Church to thrive in serving God's purpose?

In setting out to transform inherited patterns of ecclesiology and hopefully to contribute to the permanent constructive developing of a theology of the Church, I am aware of facing a strong current of denial. There is a yearning in some quarters for powerful, shiny, clear-sighted, confident smiling autocracy that in a spirit of constant optimism – and therefore without awareness of exercising subtle manipulation – minimalizes, disguises and denies that real problems are facing us, perhaps because they might seem to imply a lack of faith or disturb public confidence. Often we hear the discussion of such tough issues as though they were the personal fault or lack of strength or commitment of individuals rather than characteristics of the whole field of 'religious' activity in a postmodern context.

The picture I present in this brief report may seem overwhelmingly critical or slow to recognize the positives to be found in often hidden and fragile local church experience. But rather than taking this church temperature reading as a tabulation of gloom, I believe we should be awake to our sense of Christian confidence and well-being to recognize that a healthy and faithful Church will find courage and even humour in facing up to honest feedback. At our best we are praying to know how to be most faithful to God's vocation for us. This is to recognize both how awful it can sometimes feel, as well as how awesome, in that God's saving presence specifically allows for all our weakness and lack of insight.

This book has very much the feel of work in progress. My aim is to open up the possibilities for rethinking how we do Church together. I hope readers will have the patience to travel with me in these pages to explore the character of Church God needs us to be now. I am asking what is it possible for us to generate together now as God's Church that is not a totally integrated, closed package and yet takes faithful account of the journey of 2,000 years so far. My own journey has included interaction with many different communities of faith and the writings of those attempting to articulate hope for a Church that listens sufficiently to be serving God and God's work in all creation. They have taught me that God's Church fears neither criticism nor death and that there is a wisdom to learn about the proper balance between closing down ecclesiological agendas too soon and opening them up indefinitely. Some of the thinkers and practitioners that come immediately to mind are: Leonardo Boff, David Ford, Daniel W. Hardy, Michael Jinkins, Elizabeth Johnson, Eberhard Jüngel, Catherine Mowry LaCugna, J. B. Metz, Jürgen Moltmann, Diarmuid O'Murchu, Wolfhart Pannenberg, Michael Ramsey, Marianne Sawicki, Edward Schillebeeckx, Alan Torrance, Hannah Ward and Jennifer Wild. I write, therefore, not in a spirit of optimism but of hope and determination that, as the Church in the whole of all our living, we can learn to serve God more competently than we do at present.

CHAPTER 1

Taking Stock

Beginning with appreciations

At the start of this stocktake I want to acknowledge and appreciate the
sheer hard work, pain, endurance, sacrifice and hope implicit in the
maintenance of the local church as institution, organization, society and
community at the present time. So much of the Church's faith and life is
hidden from public view. Quietly going about their business are
thousands of laity and clergy, attempting to make faithful connections
between worship, family, work and neighbourhood responsibilities. Also,
huge numbers of laity in partnership with Readers and clergy are putting
imaginative energy into their local church's mission and life through
administration, worship and music leading, evangelism of many kinds,
education and training programmes, and fabric and finance development. In no particular order of precedence I am aware of:

- suburban and small town churches, motivated, open, solvent and
  busy;
- local churches miraculously not overwhelmed by the culture that
  regards religion as irrelevant or by often inappropriate expectations
  of standards of church maintenance and the effort to raise money for
  clergy stipends and central costs;
- teams of clergy and laity energetically dedicated to pastoral care,
  raising money for charitable projects and evangelism;
- in deprived urban areas many small churches, by their straightforward
  living out of the Good News, acting as a mainstay of the networks of
  neighbourhood survival, increasingly in the face of physical danger to
  persons and fabric;
- centres of confident and emotionally warm pentecostal worship, home
  groups of intercessors, tiny cells of contemplative prayer, careful
  preparation of Eucharist and family service, the daily offices of
  cathedrals, parish churches and individuals;
- support for Christians and their ministry in the workplace and wider
  community and, as a priority, a recognition of their work as integral to
  the mission of Christ's body, affirmed when the Church gathers for
  worship;

- university departments of theology and religious studies and learning centres for mature students offering attractive and challenging courses at many levels;
- small, scattered, rural churches, often faced with huge bills to maintain buildings and without the impetus of young people or sufficient clergy;
- experiments in prayer, music, silence, preaching, pilgrimage, and the development of the use of symbols in worship;
- the specific growth of Local Ministry Teams with varying titles and emphases;
- the commitment to radical attempts to remodel Church as an egalitarian response to God's concern for those routinely excluded by society in both urban and rural areas of relatively small numbers of clergy and laity;
- the growing yet often hidden ministry of healing;
- the exploration of industrial mission in factories, fire stations, airports and retail outlets;
- enormous care to develop excellence in child protection policies and practice;
- the occasional connection being made between church community life and the lives, thoughts and aspirations of the young;
- the pastoral and liturgical skills contributing to a generally high quality of service to society through baptisms, weddings and funerals; and
- the dedication and reflection of life in the world achieved in school, further education and higher education chaplaincies.

And yet, the clock is ticking, time is running out for inherited patterns of Church – however we look at it – theologically, spiritually, pragmatically, emotionally and financially. My observation is that, often against their own preference, most of the primary energy of bishops, archdeacons and lay administrators is consumed by the reactive round of bureaucratic activities required for the maintenance of the present Church. Conversations with regular worshippers, many of whom have reached retirement age, can reveal both a sense of anxiety that the Church will fail dramatically unless something is done and an unwillingness to see changes to inherited patterns of Church which have become a comfort in an unfamiliar world. Although it is often denied, a high proportion of stipendiary clergy in particular, at the sharp end of this crisis, is suffering stress-related illnesses. To what extent are such church leaders colluding with a culture of overwork rather than taking time to ask proactive radical questions and to model a holistic pattern as God's desire for all? How far is this acknowledged or reflected on in the light of a God who is our strength and shield, helper and refuge (Psalm 28)? So many people in churches are hurting and don't know how to let others reach out to them. How little compassion we have for ourselves and others in this critical situation. What instruments for change are available and likely to be acceptable to sufficient church members to allow for transition without total collapse?

Loss of identity

Rather than evading it, we need to focus on the sense of uneasiness that we have lost our identity as Church. The English Church Attendance Survey and interpreters such as Peter Brierley reveal to what extent the Christian Church as an organization, tested against modernity's notions of progress and growth, is in steep decline (Brierley, 2000). In many parishes and dioceses the reality of ageing congregations, the loss of young people and the lack of sufficient money to pay the clergy for the kind of Church we have inherited is causing a muted panic. A strong current of nostalgia for the days when the Church had a place in stable communities makes for an absence of clear thinking and a tendency to look for fast solutions in addressing the sharp questions that are arising.

However, there is a long tradition in Christian thinking that knows the Church and its sacraments as God's gift different in each particular place and time. We need to be alert to the significant limitations, as well as the benefits of the contributions of particular insights when taken alone. So, although it is important to hear the message of a sociologist of religion like Brierley, we also need to exercise caution regarding the restrictions of such perspectives:

> Social analysis, however, does not and cannot ask or answer theological questions. Christians must ask theological questions: at their simplest, what God is saying and doing, what words of judgement and hope there are for us in a present crisis. Otherwise we easily get locked into some kind of deterministic bondage to statistical trends or psychological processes, with little place for grace, newness, forgiveness, or freedom.
>
> (Forrester, 2000, p. 63)

A reductionist approach to images of ecclesiastical life, written in terms of marketing, commercial success or progress, can seem very thin when not held in tension with several other metaphors for Church such as servant, sign of God's Reign and hospitable community. I also believe we need to examine deeply the value of those 'successful' foundations of our Church that depend on the questionable overlay of older patterns such as Christendom, material prosperity, hierarchy and establishment.

Historians such as Alan Wilkinson (1996) and Adrian Hastings (1986) have documented the failure of institutional Christianity in Britain to read and respond to the religious needs of most of society:

> A very great deal of modern Church concern, whether of a Catholic or Protestant kind, whether it focuses on the Eucharist as the pivot of the local Christian community or on the conversion experience of the 'born-again' Christian, not only ignores but almost of necessity excludes the on-going existence of the Church's wide 'folk' periphery, the millions who are quite unlikely to be drawn in large numbers to communion or believer's baptism. The link with the periphery is, as a consequence, little served by the regular worship of ordinary parish Churches.
>
> (Hastings, 1986, p. 666)

A profound dissatisfaction with the failure of mainstream Churches, whose liberal theology could not touch the darkness and pain of existence nor provide adequate tools for describing the Church's nature and purpose, has flowed through the keen observations of theologians such as Bonhoeffer, Merton and Moltmann. The demand is for a substantial shift in our understanding of Church:

> many of the forms of embodiment and expression previously used by theology have now lost their ability to function as channels for the communication of God's love in word and deed. To put it another way: an entire constellation of beliefs, values, techniques – a 'paradigm' – is being called into question and replaced by an alternative set. If this is true for a culture, it must also become true for the religion of that culture, otherwise it might lapse into irrelevance, caught in the thought forms of a different age.
>
> (King, 1995, pp. 64f.)

The present failure of the institutional Church now is perhaps the tail end of the process that was already identified by perceptive Christians such as Karl Barth, who saw the inadequacy of liberal faith in the light of the twentieth-century wars, class warfare, the issues of unemployment and the entire disillusionment with schemes to change the world. The hurt surprise with which this demise is being greeted by many loyal church members and leaders is an indication of a lack of self-reflective awareness as a built-in element of church life. The muted outrage or lament that seems to be asking, 'What more could we have done?', 'Where did we fail you?' or 'Why won't you respond when we call?' is perhaps a consequence of living out of old assumptions for too long without really looking hard enough at the needs, pains and questions of society. This may well be the time for once powerful Churches to go quiet for a while to ponder our vocation here and now as followers of the one who came to serve and was obedient unto death.

Churches are in shock and grief that we are no longer appreciated. As a group, church members can be exceptionally sorry for ourselves. Can it really be true that the assumed pattern of ubiquitous and privileged presence in the rites of passage of most members of the population, most grand public ceremonies, most human relation contracts, and most institutions has broken down? The increasingly marginal position of the Church has been documented and disputed by sociologists long enough to raise anxiety and denial, as well as to stimulate new strategic thinking among clergy and laity. Facing this reality is a tough challenge, but doing so frees us to work on the feelings of loss and the struggle to re-imagine what God now invites us to be, with creative new energy, values and purpose in the spirit of the revelation to Julian of Norwich that 'All shall be well, and all shall be well, and all manner of thing shall be well' (see Park, 1998, pp. 78ff.).

In a new 'postmodern' world, where there is a 'profound incredulity towards metanarratives' (Lyotard in Forrester, 2000, p. 113), where 'reality and truth nevertheless come linguistically and contextually nuanced' (Patterson, 1999, p. 7) and where the atomized separation of things to discover their truth is being abandoned, what will the Church need to be like to help society discover its life in God's future? Rather than building up fast-growing, rootless congregations, authentic Christian community can be recognized in many situations as an incarnated and authentic way of living when it builds upon, and makes sense of, ordinary life here and now with its daily bread, forgiveness of sins and God's protection. Although any culture must stand under the judgement of Christ, the Kingdom that the Church must proclaim is to be worked for on earth, as in heaven. Despite the appreciations with which I began this chapter, my strong impression, gained while travelling around, is of Churches preoccupied with an obsessive struggle just to repeat the past, to survive or to offer shelter from the storm, an unchallenging place of security in which to escape the dreariness and pain of human responsibility and relation-ships.

Faced with a huge decline in ecclesiastical organization in Britain, local churches are in danger of focusing attention on fund-raising, to maintain secure inherited patterns. Attempting to get everyone into line on homogeneous belief and practice as a way of signalling to society that 'It's OK, we do really know what we're about, the message is quite simple and clear, honestly, we haven't lost the faith' can be a distraction from

Jesus' call to be as little children, open to the God of all living who invites our new engagement here and now. Reports of past performance – in belief, worship, care or witness – can sustain us but are no genuine substitute for the immediate task unfolding before us. Church press reports of some clergy attempting to impose their own 'orthodoxies' (for example, on the issues of women's ordination or human sexuality) on entire congregations to achieve political ends – such as the appointment of provincial episcopal visitors – illustrate how insular and clericalised a vision of Church some would equate with 'success' (*Church Times*, 2000).

Empirical studies of the Presbyterian Church in the USA, the Church of Scotland, Methodism and North American Reformed communions indicate the tendency of Churches under threat to adopt a survival mode and to equate mission with numerical expansion, especially among young people, to halt decline. For Anglicans in Britain there must be serious questions whether it is enough simply to take up philosophies of product appeal. There is little doubt that the general non-churchgoing public has got there before us in seeing that 'the emperor has no clothes'. In focusing on these issues we can open ourselves up to the wider field beyond those immediately around us. We can have the insights of the worldwide Church if we choose to receive from them.

Historic African Churches, founded by Westerners, now faced with a complex and worrying new society, are discovering the strength, anger and determination to change their theology and identity. Serving now as prophets and reconcilers among all interest groups, they are shedding the alien cultural forms that were forced upon them by Christian missions as a supposedly integral part of the gospel (Getui, 1999). There are black theologians writing of the courage and energy required for African Churches to recover from their colonial history and recent cases of severe mismanagement, in order to find new credibility in addressing the position of Africa's youth and women, and the growth of disease, famine and conflict. I am aware that I am treading on extremely sensitive ground here – given British history with many African countries – and yet I also recognize their experience as a present inspiration. Although the relationship between white British and black African theology contains some hugely problematic areas (Mtetemala, 1999), it is possible that Churches faced with adjusting theology and strategy could learn from the clarity and determination of twenty-first-century Pan-Africanism (Nathan, 2000). What cultural overlays will British Anglicans rejoice to cast off? What new partnerships with black Churches in Britain could assist older Churches in their search for a new identity? (see Gerloff, 2000).

I am strongly advocating the dismantling of the false dichotomy of imagining either that the Church is done for or making the assumption formed by the sharp enterprise culture that we must have firm, mono-chrome views held in place by no-nonsense, tough leadership. A key approach in this book, therefore, is the search for sustainable ways of imagining and creating conditions for face-to-face Church, communi-cating God's abundance (see Ford, 1999). How can we benevolently shape the territory we call 'Church' to better serve the brokenness and dysfunction of so much of life today? How can we improve our demonstration that we run deep enough to share the pains of all creation as well as to offer the gospel of redemption? A Church of trivial pursuits had better accept its death graciously. This is now one of the most urgent tasks of bishops and others who share church leadership: to find out how to create in the institution conditions for intimate community that will serve all God's world. Institution and community are easily set up as falsely irreconcilable opposites – institu-tion 'bad' and community 'good'. In fact the formation of an intimate Church requires routines and organizations that help make it so – this goes to the heart of the reformation of hierarchy. The choices we make continually about how to be bishops, priests and deacons are therefore vital for the character of a Church that serves the world's healing.

Although the rich concept of the 'Kingdom of God' is currently much in use, I am aware of the lack of a shared understanding among Christian Churches of the meaning of such terms. Nevertheless, God's intention for the fulfilment of the whole creation is always the Church's horizon. Although Moltmann has been accused by some of concentrating so much on the future that he neglects the need for liberation in the present, I believe his important work can help us overcome the fear that leads many Christians to a church-activity frame of mind rather one that dares to engage with all of God in all creation. He writes of the tension between defending the uniqueness of Christ and the whole of God's work in all creation, 'The real boldness of faith consists in maintaining this "deep yes to this earth" on the basis of the "passionate love of the cross and the rule of the Crucified One"' (Müller-Fahrenholz, 2000, p. 32).

A contributory factor to the Church's current pain is the centrist or localist notion that leads to a polarization of mutual suspicion. Provincial and diocesan officers for mission, ministry and education of many kinds are on the front line in experiencing this particular tension between the 'local church' – in its chaotic variety of meanings – and the so-called 'centre'. When the Bishop of Chelmsford visited his diocese in preparation for writing his Millennium Charge, a recurring message from parish clergy and churchwardens was that 'those at the centre' are a drain on our resources. One direct source of misunderstanding of the Church's nature is the growing assumption – fuelled by lack of finance – that a monochrome pattern of church polity is needed. By this I mean the preoccupation with the assumption that the Church exists only in parishes and that ideally all priests should be similarly deployed. So, for example, many whose primary calling is to be educators or reflective strategists for dioceses are placed in stressful dual-role appointments – as a means of financing their diocesan work without raising the issue in synods and governing bodies – so making lay appointments to such work very uncommon. Or those clergy who are appointed continuing ministerial education or development officers are made also vicars of huge parishes or rural deans or given responsibility for training a curate – for the sake of their credibility as 'rooted' in parochial ministry. Surely one 'important' role is enough for any of us! For limited periods say of five or six years, one focus of attention is surely sufficient for each priest – whether in a parish, a deanery, or an education and training post. If I am a continuing ministerial training officer or an archdeacon, I can be simply attached to a parish; if I am an area dean I don't need to be also on several heavyweight diocesan boards; if I accept the responsibility for training a curate, I don't need to be team rector of a huge parish.

Such thinking could help to deconstruct the notion that just a tiny group of 'hierarchy' are 'multiply important' and therefore exhausted, instead moving towards a model that looks more like a snowflake or a web with many equally significant but different parts holding it all together. Such a deployment approach would allow also for a wide range of centres of reflection and action, held in healthy tension in diocesan life. It would ensure the necessary thought required for strategic planning and the tactical development of ministries for new situations. There would be an increase in job satisfaction for more clergy (and lay leaders), and an honest recognition that, in the field of the Church, each separate place truly contributes to the whole.

Levels of anger are generated now from the misconception that every church in every place could somehow always be equally resilient, effective and financially viable. The exigencies of location and history mean that churches – like all communities – ebb and flow. Parish and diocese, local church and synod, individual and corporate, tend at present to define themselves separately and often, through perpetuating fantasies, treat each other with a naive suspicion and irritation. Conversations often reveal a puzzled and blaming sense in which everyone involved feels they have lost control of the situation and no one accepts responsibility. Often today, the naturally messy complex, interactive character of an Anglican diocese or province in all its proper diversity is ignored. In the context of a hardly spoken but widespread fear that the very existence of the Church as we know it is currently at risk we seek to identify someone to scapegoat. We imagine that if we can blame and righteously eject the one who is to blame, all our troubles will vanish. What matters more than institutional, numerical or financial survival must be the character of the Church as a true and trustworthy form of God's life in the world.

Even deeper are questions about what gospel values a reinvigorated but chastened Church would espouse. As I reflect on the post-war Church of the 1950s and 1960s when I was growing up, in contrast with the present time, there was a sense of public awareness and confidence in the local and national Anglican Church. I am thinking, for example, of Archbishop Michael Ramsey's blend of mystical, intelligent, demanding and transparent spirituality, new translations of the Scriptures selling in the high street shops, a plethora of new hymns and liturgies, excitement about the rediscovery of the work of the Holy Spirit, talk of the shaking of the foundations and the renewal of the Church, broadcast debates on morality including leading church figures, the much-publicized reforming documents of the Second Vatican Council, and the amazing phenomenon of John Robinson's *Honest to God*, publicized in the media, being widely read and publicly debated. It seemed possible then that the Church, accommodating the world view of modernity, might just be an effective player in shaping the world in the second half of the twentieth century. Perhaps the now largely forgotten report, *Faith in the City*, was the last example of that phase of history in Britain, and wrangles over the ordination of women compounded a public lack of confidence. The failure of the liberal theology approach to take with greater seriousness the conceptual richness of the Christian tradition has naturally led to a reaction. What the public experiences today is an Anglican Church frequently backed by a more conservative theology, prone to making naive declarations on human and gender relationships in a changing culture, absorbed in liturgical revisions and erring towards a patronizing ethos in evangelistic and education programmes. These are just some of the signs of a Church with very clear boundaries and a monochrome culture. In suburban settings this formula has often built up apparently confident and growing congregations but we have a constant and difficult task to test what God is asking of Churches now. What are our success criteria?

As I appreciated earlier, there are churches deeply engaged with the local community, schools, civic life and all kinds of projects to improve human living, but intelligent energy seems to be largely absent for reflecting on how to work with God's life in all of creation, especially where congregations are weary with the work of survival. From New Testament days the identity of the Church has had to be pursued along the tightrope of both listening to the world and also having a strong degree of ambivalence. Instead of a head-to-head collision course between the methodology and language of liberals and conservatives, both of them denying the reality of each other's faith, we could simply recognize that, alone, neither of them in themselves is complete or adequate. New energy seems to be flowing where there is a rigorous testing of past forms of Christian practice, authoritative beliefs and the dominant ideas and achievements of contemporary society. Remaining supremely suspicious of all forms of manipulation and domination, this ecclesiological approach learns from and engages but refuses to sit easily with techniques for building and organizing human society. This Church co-operates wherever possible with others who are engaged in fostering human flourishing but will sit uncomfortably with civic values such as noble self-sacrifice and the duty of those to whom much has been given to put out a helping hand towards the weak. If as Church we dare to struggle to find a new identity, at its heart we shall primarily need to be gripped by new insights that flow out of our taking part in the contemporary, international, ecumenical reflection on the character of God, on parts of the Christian tradition that were overlooked for much of the twentieth century, and in dialogue with a variety of rich human insights, vibrant disciplines and faith traditions. I am assuming an understanding of tradition that is a process of continuous reflection and reworking, contributed to and viewed differently by women, men, children, lay and cleric, in all times and places, which enables of myriad models of being Church.

One of the key insights that Anglicans bring to the wider questions about what is required of us as Church today is a long practice of deliberately and genuinely setting out to know the territory and peoples in which a church is set, in its complexity and plurality. Debates on the future of Christian communities need to be raised above the level of money and predictions of reductions in clergy numbers and will need to welcome the polyphony of meanings taken on by the expression 'local church' or 'ministering community' as a habitus of Christian practice, discovering what God is calling us to be and do today – in school, hospital, chaplaincy, retail outlet, prison and airport.

Anglican churches in Britain today reveal countless examples of taking trouble to identify the shape and constitution of the population of a place as a deliberate commitment to the Jesus who shows us God's involvement in all creation. What is the history of this piece of land, the development of its street names, long-standing feuds, the chequered economic history, the famous and infamous characters who have lived here, the changing population and housing patterns, the celebrations and sorrows, industrial, agricultural and commercial influences, political activities, social concerns, the comings and goings of ethnic and religious groupings and buildings, public services and transport, education, employment variations, the effects of national and international events such as wars, trading and epidemics, music and culture? When churches fail to keep up with, in order to hold a critical conversation with, the actual rather the imagined situation in which they live, the unconscious result is often to be working on a diminishing canvas. Stephen Pattison offers students and Churches a friendly approach to holding a critical conversation as a dialogical way of learning to understand and think about relationships between contexts and concepts and others (Woodward and Pattison, 2000, pp. 35, ff.).

Dioceses are currently struggling to make decisions, follow through policies, connect speeches in synods with local behaviour, keep faith with parishes, respect their officers and advisers, spell out policies, promote coherent education and training, set budgets, and collect quotas from the parishes. Mostly we have not yet found attitudes, structures and ways of debating or agreeing strategies that will facilitate such vital coherence. For example, there are leaders struggling to explain that recent changes in ministerial strategy are more due to theological issues (positive) than to the need for financial stringency or reducing numbers of stipendiary clergy (negative). Why can't we accept that the future shaping of the Church is a vulnerable and unpredictable business determined by a kaleidoscope of factors both within and outside the Church itself? This is not a matter of setting up one set of reasons in isolation from others nor of tying 'success' to a particular outcome, such as greater numbers of vocations to ordained ministry. In the absence of a complex-enough method of co-operation, a spirit of blame can easily begin to infect the spirit of everyone. One of our objectives should be to explore how there can be a greater imaginative sense of every different part of diocesan or regional church life relating to every other to promote the whole.

For leaders of large and complex church organizations to discover the need and possibilities for strategic planning when publicly faced by crises is challenging but not impossible. It happens with great frequency and as part of the natural professional development of leaders in the world of business and education. At all levels of church activity, still pervaded by the expectation of respectful subordination, we are often inhibited from creatively and honestly offering appropriate critique to senior figures. Why do we still want to lie at the feet of leaders who are above contradiction only to reject them when they cannot meet our every expectation? Along with the collusive mystique of hierarchy goes the absence of realistic ways of challenging inadequate or partial insight and skill. Continuing ministerial education for all accredited church ministers may be officially accepted, but attempting to relate it naturally to perceived need at significantly senior levels of management in the Church will take further work.

'Politeness is the poison of all good collaboration', remarked Nobel Prize winner, Francis Crick (Fullan, 1993, p. 82). I believe we hold ourselves back in church life when we don't find ways of speaking our truth with both fire and sensitivity and when we punish or ignore those who do. Bishops' staff and council meetings, synods and committees are stifled by convoluted talk with occasional staccato outbursts by brave individuals who then temporarily retire in confusion or in the long term take their passion where it can be received. Life in all its fullness is so often, apparently, not required here.

It takes a great deal of time and accumulated reflection on experience for individuals and groups to address the deep questions out of which policy is derived and for which aims and objectives can then be developed. So, what plans need to be made to enable this work of integrated future planning to happen so that the Church can learn to ask and answer vital questions about its vocation, identity and effective working patterns?

Regularly bishops and dioceses decide there must be a comprehensive survey of the parishes to see if they are being effective in mission or conforming with expressed central policies. There is a recurrent argument that dioceses are greatly assisted by having a better knowledge provided by the answers to a survey on demography, patterns of worship, mission, family structures and spirituality. Question-naires are circulated – taking many hours to complete – which aim to assess trends and statistics. Clergy and laity have long memories of the completing of such papers that are rumoured to lie unread in arch-deacons' lofts. It took just six months to complete the Domesday Survey of 1086 but that was a naked exercise of the power of Norman overlords. In fact I wonder whether such surveys can ever deliver very much of value. Unless a database is constantly updated, the information will quickly be incorrect. A diocese would need its education and training team to be focusing its energies on the outcome and potential of such a survey, as a clear and co-ordinated policy to the exclusion of other work. There would need to be more of a sense of 'diocese' as a cohesive unit than is currently experienced. The changes of clergy and laity alter the picture very significantly; and, as we know, the movements and retire-ments of bishops and the consequent vacancies and new personal policies raise many serious questions about the outcome for so much effort.

The urgent question is increasingly being raised about the distinctive role of a bishop in fostering the Church's mission. The current moves in the Church of England to open the way for the admission of women to the episcopate offers a new and exciting opportunity to revisit the Church's expectations of bishops for the kind of Church God now requires. The nineteenth-century, idealized historical picture (given credence by *Lumen Gentium* 28 in the documents of the Second Vatican Council) of bishops based directly on the order of apostles, now seems to fail to recognize the more complex processes of development that were taking place in the early centuries (see Pannenberg, 1998, p. 379). The present and particular Church's faithfulness to its history (apostolicity) and other contemporary expressions (catholicity) are the responsibility of the entire committed church membership, of which the bishop is both symbol and inspiration. But still there is a core of truth in expecting bishops in their particular role to take a significant lead in preserving the Church in gospel faith. History may show our period to have hard-working managerial bishops who feel a compulsion to be very much involved in every local church and to work for a high degree of cohesion. A bishop such as John Moorman, Bishop of Ripon in the 1960s and 1970s, clearly had a contrasting laissez-faire model of episcopacy, travelling often to his Lake District cottage to pursue his studies ('no one wants a bishop at the weekend'), spending long periods over four years as the Anglican representative throughout the Second Vatican Council and regarding his day as his own for study and writing, unless someone had made a bid for his time. Yet no one could have been more rapid and thorough in exercising pastoral oversight when it was required. I'm not trafficking nostalgia as a solution. Rather I am exposing the need for a rationale of being bishop that is theologically satisfying and works in our day. This book is not proposing a false dichotomy – either we have bishops (hierarchy) or we abandon episcopacy altogether. Chapter 3 will show how crucial bishops can be in helping to lead the Church to new patterns of mutuality rooted in the New Testament concepts of the Body, and *koinonia*. I am not naively suggesting that there ever was a golden age of egalitarian Christian community in which everyone found a place and dignity, but rather that any reconsideration of the Church's character needs to engage with the central notion of love that lies at the heart of Jesus' showing of the community of difference, in equal and different relation, that is God's own trinitarian life. It follows that it is vital for bishops (and indeed parish priests and other diocesan staff) to contribute to working out what character their leadership will need to have in this process at this moment in the Church's development in British society now.

Gerard Loughlin has presented us with the vision of a postmodernist society like an endless shopping mall in which religious customers choose the style that fits them (see Patterson, 1999, p. 8). The New Testament itself and the history of Christian divisions suggest that many partial and competing versions of Christianity coexist. My experience is that that self-deception or choosing to deal with only part of the whole picture is more common in church circles than in other social groups. In Loughlin's words, we are all 'the product of many interrelated narratives' (Patterson, 1999, p. 8). We often choose to ignore parts of the picture that do not fit our self-understanding; we give more weight to evidence that supports our view of church attendance or consistency of belief or commitment; we select our biblical passages, hymns and language for God; we choose those doctrines and insights that make sense or are personally helpful at different moments of our human story; we frequently criticize others for their personal sexual behaviour, ignoring the genuine complexity of biblical insight; and we ignore blatant communal refusal to face the demands of the gospel on world debt, torture or modern-day slavery. We could let ourselves off the hook about this in the knowledge that only the triune God has the task of holding the world together. However seductive, to locate too much unifying, rigid, monolithic authority with senior church leaders is asking more of them than a fully adequate ecclesiology or sheer common sense can allow. No single picture or formulation of words about Jesus Christ has ever existed or will ever exist, but fortunately our faith is in Christ not the coherence of Christianity and we are not Christian on our own and together in comprehensiveness God is known in Churches and in the world.

Why Church? Searching to renew our identity

Asking questions about the Church's identity and responsibility is often given lower profile than asking 'How can we do this better?' or 'How can we find a better way of doing this?' International and ecumenical debates on the Church in recent decades have helped us to understand the Church's task in terms of a 'learning community', expressing as stewards as much of the life and action of the trinitarian God as it has so far perceived. So it matters intensely how we answer the prior question, 'What God do we serve?' The Church's experience of the life-giving ways of the Spirit, the liberating power of Jesus Christ, and the mysterious, fragile energy of the Creator, reveals the one God as multifaceted. In the last few decades, in the Church of England as in other Churches there has been an undoubted shift towards a more thorough grounding of ecclesiology in the triune God, together with a fresh interest in the specific action of the Holy Spirit.

My own dialogue with John Zizioulas and Leonardo Boff in *Transforming Priesthood* (Greenwood, 2000b) helped me to clarify the life of God as an event of communion and the life of the eucharistic community as one of differentiated unity. As Zizioulas has written with rigour:

> We need to find the golden rule, the right balance between the 'one' and the 'many', and this I am afraid cannot be done without deepening our insights into Trinitarian theology. The God in whom we believe is 'one' by being 'many (three)', and is 'many (three) by being one'.
>
> (Zizioulas in McPartlan, 1993, p. 180)

It has become commonplace for parishes, bishops and synods to talk of the Church primarily in terms of sharing in God's mission. Discovering precisely the shape of this mission in society in England today and in the particularities of a given place – in other words asking what we have to do to be a godly Church here and now – is increasingly the process to which dioceses and churches are currently devoting much energy. Local churches, often in response to diocesan invitation, have taken time to write and continue revising their mission statement. With so much emphasis on the local, it is all the more important now for dioceses to have resources to help local churches make connections with radically changed understandings of mission from outside in Europe, Asia, Africa and Latin America. The tendency to see only part of the picture is reflected sometimes in a polarization in thinking of mission either in terms of disaster aid, medical work, famine relief, digging wells and running schools, or in terms of evangelism, discipleship training, spiritual development or equipping leaders. Holding together the gospel to the complete person and the whole world is a challenge for mission priorities in a fragmented world.

For the overwhelming majority of white Britons of Christian heritage educated in recent decades, religion plays an insignificant place in their lives. For a Church to speak to a nation, it seems common sense to be able to speak in many 'dialects' simultaneously in the sense that Archbishop William Temple spoke of the Church for those who do not belong to it. However, it seems to be the case that in each generation there arises, almost unconsciously, a dominant way of being Church that takes a number of issues for granted and finds it difficult to notice its partial understanding of what is going on. Archbishops Michael Ramsey, Donald Coggan and Robert Runcie in their particularity bring to mind sets of core values that for a time were dominant and taken for granted to the exclusion of others – about the character of God, God's ways of communicating, the relationship between society and Church, the significance of the whole people of God, Scripture, Eucharist, tradition, priesthood, mission and so on. At the time of writing I notice a tendency towards an anti-intellectual emphasis on a simple reading between Bible and life today, an absence of challenge to most church members of making connections between faith and everyday life – and Christian people are very willing to be sucked into churchiness, a suspicion of theological reflection, ambivalence about effective management, an emphasis on the nuclear family as an overarching model of Christian practice, a fear of different understandings of sexuality, and a reluctance to give time to thinking deeply about world issues in the light of Christian faith (see Church House Publishing, 2001, chapters 1 and 2). So what is missing? We need to identify what we are not hearing and seeing, what the dominant voices are failing to say and who they are silencing, and in our choice of leaders locally and regionally, who we are excluding and thereby making the picture too small. What other images and language would we require to be talking about Church in order to engage more fully with God who is at work in all things?

This is a key question of the vocation of the Church whether gathered or dispersed. What kind of gathering of people ('society') are local churches called to be or claim to be – for example, a collectivity for receiving ministry and worship, or a community, and if so in what sense? So, for example, in local congregations and church councils a fearful awareness is growing of being incapable of making contact with the vast majority of young people. Questions are raised such as: 'What kind of Church would we need to become for young people to find value and meaning in belonging?' 'What support can we be to young people discovering who they are in a fast-changing world?' 'What changes are we realistically prepared to make to meet young people's needs and include them in worship and decision-making, or should each age group simply have its own Church?' In 1999 the General Synod of the Church of England accepted unanimously that church schools stand at the centre of the Church's mission to the nation. What does this mean for 'local churches'? Perhaps it is no longer the Church that supports its school but the school that supports the local church. Is this such a dramatic change from, say, the flourishing Sunday-school movement of the nineteenth century when most children receiving biblical and ethical education did not regularly take part in the public worship of the parish church?

Pursuing this question of our corporate vocation, does it matter if many churches are tending to be monochrome in the particular interpretation and expression they offer of the Christian faith and in the range of culture, education, degree of wealth, and even age that choose to be regular worshippers? When we use the phrase 'people of God' to describe a local congregation, are we referring only to Anglicans? What would it mean if we honoured the spirit of the parochial system by beginning to reconfigure churches in geographical locations as thoroughly ecumenical in both membership and leadership? Ecumenical partnership in local churches and diocesan education schemes is far less consistent than the signing of formal agreements, prayer and meeting among church leaders of various traditions might suggest. Much ecumenical co-operation is in fact local and largely unknown. The evidence offered by written-up case studies shows the value as well as the vulnerability of developing co-operation between the Anglican, Baptist, Methodist, Roman Catholic and United Reformed Churches for worship, children's and youth ministries, ministry among the elderly, and in the deployment of licensed ministers.

These issues arise sharply at times of critical decision-making – say about clergy appointments, selection for training of clergy and Readers, and budget decisions – but for the most part are ignored or treated as questions for individual judgement. We need to explore what effect it has on a Church when it lurches between homogeneous uniformity and unresolved difference taken to the point of fragmentation. A loose confederation of Christian communities has lost its means of maintaining communion with Christians of other centuries, not least those of the first generations who worked through conflict to maintain a differentiated unity, as well as with partner Churches of other traditions today. Working to uncover, face and resolve hidden differences – not only for itself, but also as a sign for society – is a statement about the Church's own sense of mission.

This is also a question of polity. How does the Church we claim to be organize itself so as to implement its present, rather than outdated ecclesiological principles? Are we still committed to the parish system? Who is the Church's ministry for? What form of ecclesial authority is characteristic of the gospel and required now?

I find some of the greatest clues for a Church's identity now in a rich mixture of worship, order and spontaneity; wrestling with life of many boundaries; entering into creative, joyful power; weaving emotion with intellect; manifesting commitment to those on the edge of society and Church; giving attention to detail in care; and relishing the community life of the Society of St Francis, the Iona Community, the base church communities and the Local Ministry movement. If institutional Christianity has a future it lies in paying attention to the seeds of regeneration to be found in those provisional communities that are prepared to lose everything in discovering again how to follow Christ. We need to ask, 'What ways of being Church will best enable the resurrection life of apostolic faith to be lived, recognized, embraced and shared among the mass of people in our country in the present circumstances?' What drains energy is church life that has lost its expectation, chiefly of God. It's evident that as salt can lose its savour, Churches can live with anxiety and a dread of their own daring in a bored half-light (see Perls *et al.*, 1951, p. 413).

The set of concepts we have for understanding ourselves as Church are too important to be left to chance. They seem to determine the range of our ability to respond to the demand of God's Kingdom. If our self-understanding is inadequate we can unwittingly become false prophets. Choosing to 'be Church' in particular ways as an alternative to loyally maintaining our supposed inheritance is more than nostalgia; it can be actively to oppose Christ. A dramatic illustration that makes the point has recently been offered by William T. Cavanaugh (1998). He invites us to check the criteria we have for being 'Church' by holding up the failed ecclesiology of the Church in Chile during the Pinochet regime. Nicholas Healy well summarizes:

> The Chilean Church had adopted a European ecclesiology that prescribed a fundamentally organic relation between the nation state and the Church. The former is to deal with political matters while the latter looks after the 'soul' of the nation and avoids any involvement in the political sphere. This ecclesiology of harmony prevented the Church from recognising that its own central practice, the Eucharist, conflicted radically with the practice of torture that had become central to the Pinochet state.
>
> (Healy, 2000, p. 48)

Although the two-tier paradigm does have an internal logic, in that context it disabled the Church from truly serving God's Kingdom for the sake of 'these little ones'.

Local Ministry – otherwise referred to as Total, Common or Mutual Ministry – is continuing gradually to redefine the mission and ministry of the local church. Over recent decades in the majority of dioceses, Local Ministry in many differing ways has been developed as a focus for the language of and experiments in collaborative ministry. As Daniel W. Hardy suggested when speaking at a meeting during the 1998 Lambeth Conference, like a 'gusher' that allows deep reservoirs of new fuel to be brought effectively to the surface and converted into usable energy, Local Ministry has the potential for helping Churches to rediscover themselves in a new set of human contexts and against the background of profound shifts in theological emphasis. As I shall explore in later chapters, although initial prophetic energy for this movement has been assertively and consciously reshaping local ministries, experience suggests that in the future it is likely to be more productive where energy is expected and allowed to run locally and unpredictably in response to the original generative ideas.

Where there is concentrated attention given to prayer by a high proportion of a church community, institutional problems fade. There are thousands of Christians in Britain following a personal prayer discipline, involved in intercession and silent prayer groups, saying a daily office corporately, praying the Eucharist in the week, and learning to be more effective spiritual guides. But in my experience as one who visits many different churches in the course of a year, many church members are not being encouraged either to pray or to think for themselves. The energy of the laity will always be disengaged if attention is given only to the surface, practical routines of church activity. When the ecstasy of a deep prayer life for Christians is not taught, encouraged or fostered as a matter of course, love for God and for others is bound to run dry and the Church's problems become insurmountable. Further, none of us can dare to make necessary changes in understanding of style of life unless our thought and prayer have been allowed to run deep. It is a task of church leadership to make normal provision in church routines for intimacy with God and with one another. When we assumed the task of Church to belong primarily to clergy and a few pious laity we made the appropriate educational and spiritual arrangements for that elite few. Now that we are learning to see that each person has a vocation in God's plan, we shall logically need to make alternative arrangements so that everyone can be lifted into their vocation appropriately.

There is an immense amount of work urgently to be done in redesigning forms of adult Christian education offered by parishes and dioceses. Education – its processes and content – forms the Church continually, so our choices need to be made in responsible awareness. There is currently a false dilemma, which contrasts education provided to prepare a few individuals for particular public ministries with education as a general and dynamic stimulus for committed Christian living. Why can't we have both, as needed? In practice most courses, however flexible, are designed for quite a narrow range of mental and personal types. I have seen many people in Britain aspire to complete them, some exceeding their dreams and others quietly accepting defeat. Such an approach continues to create a homogeneous, middle-class, élitist, dependent Church rather than 'a kind of parallel community which represents a challenge to the secular order because it stands as an alternative possibility of ordering life' (Forrester, 2000, p. 193).

Learning organization thinking has been influencing large complex companies for several years but has hardly made an impact in Church circles. The underlying proposition is that all organizations need education that supports individuals and the organization itself in a time of rapid change. To flourish in such a context requires members and the organization as a whole to adopt a stance of continuous learning, and learning of a sophisticated kind. In *Becoming a Learning Organisation*, Swieringa and Wiersema propose that the 'challenge is to create an organisation capable of rapid and continuous change' (1992, p. 3). So it is no longer adequate for any organization to rely merely on individual skills-training, or on the assumption that there is a simple, correct solution to every problem. A theology of Church rooted in the baptismal calling of the whole people of God requires us to pay attention to the wisdom of the 'learning organization' and to offer to all Christian adults holistic opportunities for continual transformation.

> Christ has invited the entire church to walk, speak and serve in the world. Education dare not be measured in pages finished, books completed, people in attendance. Learning needs to lead to meaning and understanding but even this, if an end in itself, is meaningless.
>
> (Everist and Nachtigal, 1997, cited in Walker, 2001, p. 6)

Total Ministry parishes in New Zealand engage in a process in which enablers are supported to produce or find the material that best suits where they are working. Originally, they followed the Nevada programme designed for diverse (isolated rural, central city, suburban, Anglo-Catholic, Evangelical, large and small) situations and could not produce material to suit them all. Enablers have gradually proved themselves creative and keen to develop material for particular localities. The Local Ministry Officer in Christchurch, Jenny Dawson, reports:

> We are very clear that training and formation is for everyone not just the Ministry Support Team – and it is obvious that our Total Ministry parishes have a much higher participation rate in studies and training than other parishes. We don't have a specific curriculum.

In Britain we need to question inherited adult education patterns especially in the light of the growth of Local Ministry. We shall need to plan – regionally, ecumenically, using many creative educational insights together – for the kind of variety of opportunities locally that will stimulate a wide spectrum of people in their desire to know and serve God in the whole of life. Education is a key element in the growing of a Church that understands itself corporately as having a vocation to collaborate in God's total work:

> It cannot consist simply in the learning of what could be called arcane knowledge and practice. It must provide the means for discerning the work of God in today's world, by all the possibilities which faith and modern critical scholarship afford ... All of us, and certainly theological education, need to be awakened to the task of discerning the work of God in today's world.
>
> (Hardy, 1996, p. 224)

There is often an assumption that God communicates mainly or chiefly through the Bible, or certain parts of it, so that the opportunities for learning from the God-inspired disciplines and insights of cosmology, biology, science, literature, music and art – the negative, ugly and destructive as well as the positive, beautiful and creative – are ignored. Education programmes can give the impression that learning about discrete topics such as religious language, liturgy, history and ideas is a valuable end in itself. Another answer to the question 'Why Christian education?' may point more to 'How do I learn more effectively to read God's presence and will, so that I can work with God for the coming of the Kingdom?' Abandoning notions of lifelong learning, there seems at present to be a danger of overloading those preparing for particular ministries by offering them a rushed and watered-down summary of a traditional degree in theology. Although separate topics may be addressed – such as ethics, worship, history, Bible and doctrine – there is an absence of cohesion or formation for the particular ministry in question. For example – in relation to the work of Timothy Jenkins to be discussed in Chapter 2 – how do bishops, clergy and lay leaders learn more about the skills of understanding the complexities of a location, community-building or discernment without which their work is naive and limiting? Of course dioceses have limited resources of finance and tutors, so all the more reason to examine why they are providing education and with whom they could be co-operating. Some Local Ministry Schemes initially adopted quite rigid educational approaches and are constantly reviewing them in the light of experience.

The Church's identity now as a foretaste of God's desire for the identity of all creation requires the recognition and development of a wide differentiation of ministers in partnership. There is in Local Ministry a huge but, as yet, largely untapped opportunity for local churches to introduce learning at many levels – interweaving disciplines, thought and feeling; allowing equal dignity for all educational needs and skills – for communities and individuals at every stage of life. The particular work of bishops and archdeacons is not to leave this to chance but help to form considered strategies and deployment policies to nurture the conditions in which a true diversification of ministry can flourish.

Developing a Church of diversified ministries

I want to argue with rigour that this transitional period in which the Church has partly lost its way can be recognized as exciting, liminal and challenging, though difficult and personally risky, requiring deep wells of prayer and reflection. There is a dawning realization that there is no consolation that it will soon be over and a new stability will take the place of change. Our present practice resonates strongly still with the Middle Ages, which centred the faith and worship of parish, cathedral, chapel, college, large household and diocese in clerics of various kinds (Legood, 2000, p. 131ff.). In seeking to become a missionary Church not entirely dependent on clergy and bishops, we have to confront another false dichotomy – namely, the challenge that a church of everyone in their everyday work threatens Anglican polity, especially by denying the value of ordained ministry. Church leaders have to take a persistent lead in teaching that we are exploring a new form of partnership, which the sixteenth-century Reformation failed to achieve. When there is no consistent, thought-through approach, Churches get stuck with limiting questions like, 'Who is allowed to preach, to take services, to give communion, to walk in front of whom in the procession?' and so on. This reinforces a self-limitation and reveals a Church obsessed with regulations, status and suspicion of experimentation. Faced with radical change, the attitude, 'I can't find what you're suggesting on any page in the Constitution' has to be challenged. If Churches are intrigued with internal arguments about who is responsible for what and putting limits on people's power, the chances seem slim of reaching a mature, fresh understanding of Church that resonates with what we know of God's mission now and can satisfy the needs of society and individuals.

Once when I was leading a workshop, and attempting in diagrams to explore future possibilities for a collaborative Church, I had the back-row comment, 'If you can't draw it, how can we do it?' This is a key issue. We are all invited now to become part of the debate, which must not be closed down too soon. No one alone has the answer. We are called to work together, offering our various insights and listening to what each knows of God. As I shall explore in the final chapter, this is more about meditation together than mechanical technique.

In our heads we know the Church is not centred in the clergy as if they were religious experts, the equivalent of the aristocrats of past centuries. A key to reading the context of church life now is the 50 years or so of reawakening of a sense of Church as a diversified community in service to God's Kingdom, which includes the equal but various ministries of all, that we have been experiencing. All the players in the Church's life have a certain role to fulfil as well as being deeply reliant on one another. The movement of the Spirit that reaches out from the Second Vatican Council, the Lima Texts of the World Council of Churches, many ecumenical negotiating documents, the writings of theologians and the centres of pioneering practice has the power to transform the idea of the Church from that which has been inherited. The difference is clear to see in terms of lay confidence, transformed clerical practice, and the development of mission as central to local church life where such connections have been taught and practically developed.

So, habitually we offer great honour to bishops, priests, and deacons, but we need to ask again, for what? To whose expectations are they working? Conversations and observations reveal a paradox. Many clergy are reacting violently against inherited patterns of assimilating the ministry of all or acting in the place of Christ and allowing others to have a merely derived ministry, so that they offer nothing distinctive from other Christian ministries. Others react, consciously and unconsciously, against recent attempts to transform understandings of priesthood and disable others by holding on to all authority and decision-making. For example, the model of visiting consultant continues to be espoused by both clergy and bishops. Imagining that by ordination they are chosen and equipped to know what the whole reality of the Church should be, such clergy take on the role of doctor to an ailing patient, the local church. As if they could be a detached observer, they diagnose the illness and prescribe and deliver the appropriate remedy.

What emerges is a picture of the diocese in which the task of the parish priest is being interpreted in diverse ways with a reluctance to examine these differences. The diversity could be seen as a response to the difficulty the Church now experiences in seeking to satisfy dependency needs in society while moving towards a more collaborative model of Church. In the absence of an agreed strategy, there is bound to be huge stress for individuals attempting to find ways of coping with the uncertainty and to know whether they were being affirmed. The diocesan organization generally and the fragmented arrangement of education and training in particular have the function of allowing the individual member of the clergy to feel that their own way of coping is, if not positively endorsed, at least tolerated and certainly not threatened or opposed.

Working hard to identify the range of meanings of priesthood in the Church now is an urgent task and one too important to be left to clergy and professional theologians alone. Of course we expect someone who gives all or some of their working life to ordained ministry to have something particular to contribute to the community out of their privileged time for prayer, study and wrestling with issues of life and death. And, of course, no one expects clergy to have an answer, even the 'correct' answer, to every question we may have about God. Learning to hold the truth in several different ways simultaneously may be a clue to the future patterns of Church and ministry that faithfully echo God's own life.

As has already happened to doctors, academics and lawyers, increasing pressure is taking a toll on the lives of priests. There is an uncomfortable and almost unspeakable paradox here, that ministers of grace, peace, reconciliation and the gospel of resurrection have not on the whole found the resources to face the conflicting demands that confront them. These are laid on them one way or another by the unchallenged expectations of 'the hierarchy', peers and congregations; changing expectations about status and authority in both Church and society; a greater accountability, especially in professional conduct; negativity and suspicion in the press; past role models; new theories; the growing expectation that each priest will do more work; a high degree of mismatch between people and jobs; the desire of married clergy to take more part in the raising of their children and to be creative in relating to their spouse; and perhaps most of all the demands they place upon themselves.

A significant proportion of clergy experience depression and illness when faced with unresolved conflicts in prioritizing possible avenues of work against a background of severe cutbacks among the full-time ordained. I observe many clergy striving to maintain loyalty to old patterns of parochial ministry when they are the only priest in several parishes. Politeness, overwork and misplaced kindness among arch-deacons and bishops often seem to inhibit their proper and direct critique of this situation. Affirmation of everyone unless they break the law is not the leadership we need. The pressure is set to increase as laity – increasingly aware of paying the bills – are becoming less content with hierarchical and non-consultative decision-making. For ordained women there continue to be singular stresses related to the holding of two integrities in the Church of England, the very varied response to women's ordination in congregations and society, and unresolved status and power issues both in terms of diocesan and national appoint-ment processes, as well as at the everyday level with male colleagues and parishioners. Much weight will rest on the degree to which a priest is supported by (and able to receive that support from) senior colleagues, peers and congregation and to which she is part of the debate about the future of the Church's mission and ministry, and how far she regards herself as a victim of circumstances, isolated in both role and personal life.

Arrival liturgies for parish priests, deans and bishops usually give the impression that the new person in charge is actually responsible for everything but may devolve certain tasks to individuals and groups. Such liturgies usually involve the person to be appointed and welcomed making a ritual territorial procession around the church building (later to be mirrored in the geographical territory of parish or diocese) to take up ownership and show who's boss. There are attempts to address this – for example, in a parish where the bishop already recognizes a Ministry

Leadership Team – but there is plenty of evidence of newly appointed clergy simply refusing to work with the structures of lay partnership previously put in place.

Although many church documents and informal communications now distance themselves from notions of a diocese governed by a hierarchy of bishops, deans, archdeacons and clergy, our true colours are often shown in the symbolism of a formal occasion – at every level of church life. With variations of personnel, this wry description of conscious/unconscious 'knowing our place' could well be a church procession anywhere in Britain today:

> Reaching the Church steps they all pause, smiling invitingly at the senior wife present. She, with a little gesture of surprise, climbs the steps ahead of them and disappears through the green curtain, leaving her inferiors to follow, quite by accident, the order of succession which protocol, had they cared about such things, would exactly have demanded.
>
> (John le Carré, 2000, p. 40)

The detailed choreographing for the welcoming of a new bishop or the licensing of Readers in a cathedral brings out the 'true' statement of how we believe 'things really are'. Cathedrals, mostly designed in the Middle Ages, despite the introduction of nave altars, expressly display an overall linear ordering of ascending power from laity to prelate. This was the character of the Church for which they were created. It takes considerable thought to work out how a diocesan gathering could express the many different leaderships and authorities of a collegial nature without simply separating off a few more 'important' people from the rest. Concentration of experiment in this area by precentors and those who devise worship will be an expression of radical commitment to collegiality in that we express our truest beliefs in our orchestrated communal activity.

A further example of this can be pinpointed in the recurring desire to add to the existing ministerial hierarchy – in a linear succession of importance – even more individual categories of commissioned persons for evangelism, pastoral work and so on. And how insulting to justify this complacently with the remark 'and yes, even the hall cleaner's work [implied, at the bottom of the heap of church work] is a vocation'. Has the speaker troubled to enquire of the hall cleaner what else might be going on in their life – family, neighbourhood, prayer or thought – that is that deep engagement with God we call vocation? It will be an important task later in this book to explore more deeply the radical possibility that in God's Church, although we may work and lead on different geographical scales, no one *in reality* can be more or less important than anyone else.

> Diversity of gifts and functions does not lead to diversity of worth, esteem or status. The work of Christ has established an equality which must be clearly expressed in the life of the church. Without equality, oneness and peace true Christian fellowship is impossible.
>
> (Forrester, 2001, p. 99)

How can we demonstrate that in practice? What will be the patterning or ordering of Church that best echoes in the patterns of its relationships the energy of God for us in Jesus Christ, dispersed in every time and place through the Spirit?

Are we merely concerned with tasks or is a renewed, relational understanding of ontology (being) possible or desirable? In the light of our mission, what patterns would be desirable? How will appropriate ordering that takes us beyond the limits of hierarchy be chosen and made provision for?

The responsibility of leaders in re-envisaging church life

The debate on what leadership is required, and how this relates to management, is currently taking up a great deal of church energy. Management is often misinterpreted as uncontrolled bureaucracy rather than a tool for releasing energy for effective, hard and satisfying work. Confusion about leadership roles has unfortunately damaged the effective handling of authority in some parishes and dioceses. Priests and bishops, shying away from former autocratic styles, often fail to offer leadership and the resultant power vacuum can result in immobility, blame and frustration. Much work is needed now to explore how the many leaderships within the Church's organization can be held together by the overall leader, given freedom, encouragement, trust and where necessary inhibition.

In an increasingly complex society, the need is emerging for a kaleidoscope of equal but different ministries. Rather than expecting a pluralism of ministries to happen pragmatically, how is this to be related to the vocation and polity of the Church? How do we critique the growth of many and various schemes and strategies employed by dioceses to stimulate the ministry of the whole Church through Ministry Teams consisting of laity, Readers and clergy? What would be the particular role of a stipendiary priest in a large cluster of settlements, served by several such Ministry Teams? What education and training would best serve such situations? Given that mission and ministry elide in Local Ministry, how do the wider structures of the Church relate to this development? Many dioceses have spent much energy espousing one form or another of partnership in ministry. Most now have advisers in Local Ministry to negotiate the details in a given context for the preparation, selection, training and development of teams composed of laity, Readers and clergy.

Some dioceses have made some form of Mutual Ministry a key element in their vision and strategy. They have invested human and financial resources in working on the important exercise of strategic planning. This involves recurring rounds of consultation and effective communication to achieve general and financial support for strategies. With cuts in public funding, some Churches have learnt that money will be forthcoming when a critical mass of people are committed to clear policies with which they can identify, which excite them and which involve them as participants locally.

Some have appointed Development Officers specifically to work systematically with the laity and clergy in parishes and deaneries, the bishops, archdeacons and other education and training officers. Experience shows that this is never an easy path and needs excellent supervision and overt support within the public structures because of the deep resistances to change the Church's culture. However, there are more chances of energy being released for progress where there is insight and willingness for the senior clergy of a diocese to collaborate on a daily basis with Development and CME Officers, precisely because the required changes affect every part of the system – appointments, review, ongoing training, deanery plans for mission, and the commissioning and development of local ministry teams.

Where there are teams of educators and trainers, experience shows that bishops and synods will be better served when they take time to set up and review the lines of authority, communication and everyday working. The national network of diocesan Ministry Development Officers has taken note of the many occasions when, despite their often considerable experience and the expertise for which they were appointed, there can be considerable resistance to allowing them to be sufficiently part of the whole picture with area deans, lay chairs, bishops and archdeacons to manage change coherently. Fortunately there are some exceptional circumstances, which demonstrate just what can be achieved through a genuine and trusting partnership where there are experiments in what it means to exercise leadership among equals. On the question of achievement, it is noticeable that Churches usually are quick to notice their shortcomings and slow to value and celebrate when goals have been reached.

Those dioceses that came early to formal Local Ministry schemes, possibly revised in the light of initial experiences and the expectations of individual bishops, tend to have a sophisticated commitment and delivery of programmes. Experience shows that where a particular bishop and a particular set of diocesan officers and diocesan committees have been willing and able to match each other in vision and energy, real progress has been made.

There are dioceses that have come more lately to Local Ministry as a formal way of promoting clerical-lay partnership for local mission. A subtle blend of financial and resourcing pressures has led to such dioceses planning to leapfrog the formal schemes approach, talking instead of a strategy through the diocese that is flexible and simply part of the bloodstream. Where there is a distinction between management and executive functions, there is the possibility of holding the authority, shaping and accountability between bishops, archdeacons, training officers, area deans and lay chairs in creative tension with the actual work of facilitation, training and co-ordination.

The images of following a seam of precious metal or of coal, or of tracers reaching up to meet lightning remind us of the immense possibilities when there is a delicate balance between order and freedom. There is much energy that goes nowhere but is hardly wasted in the probing to see what should happen next, as well as energy that is locally generated, running deeply and productively.

Evidence suggests, however, that the energy required to move the culture away from clerical dependency will not be available in a sufficiently focused way unless bishop, synod, education team, local clergy and laity deliberately set out to articulate, be aware of and foster methods for promoting Local Ministry, in many forms, as the new way of delivering the normal ministry of the diocese. This will mean taking sufficient time to debate and write a policy document on the mission and ministry of the diocese, against which all other proposals (financial, educational, staffing) can be matched. It will mean taking trouble to re-examine the ministerial theology, practice and attitudes of existing clergy of several generations as well as of those who arrive in the diocese from elsewhere. The implications – in terms of strategy, concerted policymaking and reviewing, time and energy – of undertaking this cultural shift cannot be overstated.

There are clear parallels with area or rural deans who have huge potential to release or inhibit energy in local churches. Is the deanery an appropriate size and shape? Whatever the method used for selecting the person, does the area dean have the natural confidence, the sense of permission and enough of the diocesan vision for mission and ministry to be truly effective? Does the area dean have the goodwill of the laity and clergy to have permission to do the job? Is the job well enough spelled out and agreed? What proportion of the person's overall working time is expected to be spent on being area dean? What human, financial and training resources are available and communicated to the area dean?

The Church of England now has more licensed Readers than clergy. Many are finding a more confident role through being members of a Local Ministry Team and through being encouraged to see themselves as evokers of ministry in others. Many still are fighting their corner, feeling marginalized by local clergy or not understood or respected by laity. Readers themselves, despite often experiencing a sense of isolation, can seem to others to be a perpetuation of hierarchy. Faring better than deacons – as individual, robed public ministers – they are 'allowed' to do what more senior ministers are not available or willing to do. To show commitment to and true care for Readers, the Church needs to be more rigorous in selection, including Readers in all its thinking about new patterns of partnership. Initial and continuing courses for Readers often seem isolated from various Christian studies courses, ministerial skills enhancement and ordination training. The future demands tough work on integrating all such training both as a preparation for and as a demonstration of the integration of different but equal Christian ministries.

The ecumenical education and training consortia of some regions offer exciting possibilities for the future support of ministerial training. However, quality work has to be adequately supported, financially and structurally, wherever it is based. Some dioceses are attempting to retain the status quo as well as to remain solvent by freezing full-time posts. Given the present way of being Church, the pressure to replace full-time clergy is inevitably huge – this is the way we run the Church, by having enough clergy – and bishops give in to those who make most noise. The current trend in the Church of England towards focusing all available funds in the provision of parish clergy is an icon of the lack of awareness of the urgent need for sustained investment in high-quality development and educational work to ask and answer deeper questions about the Church as an agent of change, personal transformation and conversion, and the attempt to see all life in the perspective of the Reign of God. The individualistic, inward-looking and nostalgia-driven reaction against a corporate and multidimensional approach to ministry seems paradoxically very likely to accelerate the demise of the Anglican Church in Britain in anything like its present form.

Spirituality and worship as keys to the Church's future

In my own experience, whenever membership of and excitement about new possibilities in the Church are around, they are usually linked with

prayer, silence or worship that have been designed to encourage liberation. As some clergy will occasionally out of frustration proclaim that
they can only belong to the Church if they're running it, it may be true
that most clergy and many laity only find satisfaction from, or even
attend, worship they themselves lead. It may be that the whole desire to
move to ways of being a local church that allow for immense difference is
endemically frustrated by the collusion that allows clergy to recruit like-
minded people to build up churches of their own conceiving. This is to
deny that the Church does not create itself but is the community of the
new covenant, rooted in the gifts of God and especially the celebration of
the Eucharist.

My observation is that the presentation of public worship is the chief
way in which Churches reveal their self-limitation and stem the flow of
potential energy. Anglican worship, despite the best endeavours of
liturgical revisers and the recent arrival of *Common Worship*, fails to
arrest the attention of most of the population. Even where clergy have
abandoned robes and replaced hymn books with an overhead projector,
worship can be oppressively monochrome, encouraging passivity,
inviting little depth of imagination or thought and deliberately
avoiding risk or profundity. The fact that occasional worship – at
conferences, in renewal groups, summer rallies, quarterly ecumenical or
benefice gatherings, and at Churches that make worship a priority for laity
and clergy – can be varied, inspiring and an experience of pilgrimage,
makes the point that regular worship locally is given a low-energy
priority.

This low input and expectation of energy is due to a number of factors
playing against each other, including: the pressures on clergy to take
time over other things; the lack of training of laity who are often left to
lead non-eucharistic services; the use of worship to force conformity to
one perspective on Christian belief and practice; the lack of honest and
regular informed critique, and an overall lack of daring. In particular,
worship that arrests the free enquiry of God's people and makes no
connections with their children, work and responsibilities in their raw
ordinariness comes well below an acceptable standard.

Buildings play a highly significant part in this. In my experience,
however inadequately shaped, acoustically effective, heated or lighted
it may be, the majority of local church members form a close attachment
to their particular building. This comes acutely into the foreground when
suggestions are made for closure or redesigning the worship space. There
are many exceptions, such as where huge nineteenth-century barn-like
buildings have been successfully converted for a multiplicity of purposes;
where towers, galleries and vestries have been converted to make
warmer, more serviceable spaces; where meeting rooms serve the wider

neighbourhood through the week; and where the dynamics of nave and chancel have been transformed to create worship 'in the round'.

Where there is confidence to follow the example of former generations and use the building creatively, despite the nostalgic concerns of heritage preservers, worship can be a genuine vehicle not only for our personal and corporate expression of love for God but for physically becoming a Church that is a body of people who can be intimate as well as distant with each other. The popular rediscovery in the past few decades of the worship of the early Church, which has been fed into liturgical renewal, and an emphasis on initiation rites, has raised questions of correct belief and practice but has not, except in the hands of rare practitioners, brought new life.

Clergy and laity mostly seem not to give public worship, whether on Sunday or some other day, their best or most confident attention. Yet it is often recognized that public worship transparently reveals the shape of the Good News that the local worshipping congregation believes. It also provides the main cradle in which the hopes and practice of Christian life are formed. Again many issues come together here about how the local church is led, inspired, taught and brought into a wider frame of awareness. Here is both our greatest opportunity and our greatest failure.

My experience is often of many hymns that do not speak to me now, in terms of theology, life today, gender bias or syntax. I know, occasionally, when I'm getting words and music that speak to my core and make connections with God and the world now. These are not the comments of a Philistine towards Latin motets, eighteenth-century anthems, iambic pentameters or scriptural choruses. It's more an urgent sense that it matters that we strengthen our imaginations by expecting the best use of thought, music, drama, space and language that we can achieve to speak of God's work among us here and now and our part in that. It is no coincidence that some of the most joyful and stretching worship to be conceived and performed is linked with calling human beings to their proper dignity in society and world. I have found a particular depth in the use of silence which, unusual in our culture, requires huge quantities of courage and support. Also I appreciate the gradual recognition in some quarters that to sing psalms of lament, as well as of praise, expands our capacity to relate to God in the whole of living. I see new hope where groups of laity and sometimes clergy are coming together in a parish church or some other public place, each day or week. Perhaps they ring the church bell, simply assign tasks for readings, and prayer, sometimes use simple unaccompanied musical settings, and find that they are attracting others either tentatively to join them or to ask for intercessions to be offered.

Unless we have profound worship that touches the depths, churches will continue to die. Can we dare to be Church that sees God's life already among all people and offers living worship that deals in love, laughter, forgiveness, resurrection, and not merely in words? Can we know God now in music, waiting, touching, mourning, being formal and informal, celebrating, playing – among all ages – walking, stillness, water, wine, fire, smoke, stone, light, cold and heat, feeling weakness and power, knowing God and not knowing, loving and hating, fasting and feasting? Or is that all too much to expect?

So what shall we do about this now in the roles we have already been assigned? There is an urgent need to explore how worship can make healthy connections between our hope of what the Church can be for the whole of God's world, the values and relationships our belief in God imply, and the variety of music, word, silence and movement that can on different occasions be apt.

Conclusion

In the taking-stock process of this chapter, I took care to state my awareness and appreciation of the commitment, hard work and a desire to create attractive and serving church communities. However, at the same time I have suggested we also need the confidence to recognize the disabling power of a culture of restrictive hierarchical power. It brings with it blame, and a fear of shifts in understanding God, God's mission, our part in that as Church and in a pluralism of ministries. I have portrayed a church structure that often reveals fragmentation in human relations and strategies, partial perceptions kept separate from each other, static and mechanical concepts proving inadequate to respond now to society. Almost unspeakable is the hard reality that between members and leaders of Christian communities there is not only love, respect and affection, but also misunderstanding, competitive ambition, polarized desires for the Church's future, jealousy, envy and even hostility. I have already expressed my sense of the need to discover a radically different way of being the Church now, a Church that subversively breathes the air of the whole of the trinitarian God's creative and redeeming life in every part of society, world and cosmos.

How do we know and act upon what the Spirit is saying to the Churches now? The balance of opinion in the Church now may, in fact, be to attempt to preserve the past at all costs – and this means choosing to employ clergy to make the Church happen for us as we think we have always been accustomed. Attend to the implicit verbal and performance messages at induction services that the new vicar will hit the spot; examine adverts for new clergy that speak of 'supportive laity'; and hear the 'if only' exasperation expressed at conferences, equally by laity of their vicars and by vicars of their laity.

Even if theologically we should or could, we can't afford to be the Church we were. Bishops' councils, synods and church councils often fail to recognize the unethical approach underlying the determination to continue to employ more clergy and laity than can really be afforded. Initial and continuing education and training, housing, sabbaticals, professional supervision, stipends and pensions are expensive items. We need to ask how much of this we are honestly prepared to afford and therefore what implications this has for the Church that is an expanding and generative response to God's mission in the world.

My general impression through contact with many different local churches is of a keenness to make necessary changes once there has been some real opportunity for reflection, assessment and debate, which is often best facilitated by someone with a sensitive but demanding approach. I believe there are thousands of local churches where the core membership long for a deep change of climate, attitude and practice of ministry in the widest perspective of Churches instead of the dread of our own daring that is characteristic of those whose church allegiance is more instinctive and less reflective. Yet I hope we are learning also that it would be simply to replace one top-down hierarchy with another to try to 'sort it all out' with one overarching grand plan. If the Holy Spirit deals dynamically with each person, locality and part of creation uniquely, we must rather make provision for each person to make their contribution to a paradigm shift – neither 'top-down' or 'bottom-up' but movement of an order we do not yet know how to speak of. This will be the primary creative act by which we shall make finer and in the end faster progress – to give patient, sustained attention to the entire field of current confusion rather than to blueprints or solutions.

CHAPTER 2

Seeing the Whole

One of the recurring conclusions arising from the stocktaking exercise of the previous chapter is the frequency with which the Church sets itself up to be irrelevant and peripheral. We continue to work with language, concepts and practices that together create representative pictures of the identity of God, religion, ministry and Church that are self-limiting. One notable example is our persistent rootedness in a doctrine of individualism, dominated by incipient clerical control of the Christian community. Another is to place ourselves beyond the comprehension of most ordinary human life and agendas. In particular I have in mind those aspects of local church assumptions and practice that deliberately: displace the work of the people of God by clergy and bishops as though this were a fundamental gospel truth; place emphasis on the solitary individual finding salvation and the assurance of God's love in isolation; make only reluctant connections between the experience of worship and everyday responsibilities; fail to support people in the diversity of their everyday working roles; are inward-looking or claim to read God's Word exclusively from the Bible; ignore the complexity of life in the world now by working in step-by-step linear ways; separate the life of the Church from complex contemporary pointers about leadership and management; and cut themselves off from Churches that take different perspectives.

When we anxiously exhibit these characteristics we have forgotten our vocation to be constantly learning, in order to be:

> a polymorphic cloud of witnessing communities whose shapes change with the times and locales, the winds, and other atmospheric necessities, a plurality of communities in different contexts, being sacred traditions often at variance with other communities of faith.
>
> (Jenkins, 1999a, pp.3f.)

Timothy Jenkins invites Churches to welcome the gravitational pull of particularity and plurality as 'play at work' – which recent researches into the earliest forms of Christian faith and community are also discovering (see Jinkins, 1999, p. 4). Another way of expressing this is to talk of Churches enjoying a process of learning, in order to be prophetically committed to making active contributions to the general building up of wider society through cultural, ecological, economic, political or social processes in ways that echo God's life and character (see Hawkins, 1997). Learning here is not the drawing together of data or expert knowledge about things, but a commitment to deepening our ways of perceiving how the world in God is dynamically ordered as complex difference and unity and therefore how we might respond as a Church that serves God's mission. Christian wisdom is the mapping out of possibilities for living in this world in the ordering of the God whose ways are revealed in Christ.

The tendency toward separating out God and faith from the mainstream of living produces a dangerous foundation for a version of Church, placidly retreating from the world rather than staying with and offering hope and challenge to society. Forgetting Jesus' words, 'I came to bring fire to the earth, and how I wish it were already kindled' (Luke 12.49), the Churches are mostly giving up on the claim that Christ's death and resurrection reveal the love of God everywhere and the passion of God for the whole world's future.

This is to forget the task of the disciple to imitate Christ's stand against principalities and powers by taking part in the eschatological work of disarming 'the rulers and authorities' and making 'a public example of them, triumphing over them in it' (Col. 2.15). The word '*eschaton*' means end, the end of this age and of the history that runs its course in it (Rev. 10.6–7). In Christian eschatological expectation, the rising of Christ from the dead in theological discourse today is vigorously linked with the concept of the Kingdom of the triune God to anticipate the reconciliation of individuals and societies and the consummation of God's hope for all creation (see Pannenberg, 1998, pp. 580ff.). For Zizioulas the Church lies more in the future than in the past. It is certainly a product of its history, but in the celebration of the Eucharist, the Church already begins to know itself as it will be finally created by the Spirit. So the eucharistic community, in all its present failure and confusion, is also an icon of the Kingdom, announcing what is to come. Each Christian in the local church is not only part of a historically constituted Church, but through the Eucharist can already begin to know herself as reconstituted through the perfecting work of Christ. As witnesses, Churches are provisionally called to know and reach their true potential in order to show the world how life might be, by demonstrating in its own existence how to be free:

> The Church of the martyrs saw itself as a 'contrast society', a holy people called out of darkness to be a light to the nation (1 Peter 2:9), a people who rejected the sword and practised justice and charity not

only among their own but among strangers and their pagan neighbours.

(Cavanaugh, 2000, p. 63)

This chapter will challenge these false separations by beginning to suggest foundations for imagining an irreducibly pluralist Church that dares to claim that the horizon of faith and of practical Christianity is never less than the whole of God's life as triune communion in the reciprocal complexity of the universe. Sue Patterson rightly claims, 'our knowledge of God is not confined to the overtly religious but is present in all truth' (Patterson, 1999, p. 2). The gospel of Jesus opens up the promise of God's Kingdom precisely in terms of words and stories about relating, buying and spending, employing and firing, extending and withholding compassion and hospitality, marrying and divorcing, raising children, paying taxes, health and disease, use and misuse of authority, and the whole of existence (see Dunn, 1992).

The vast majority of people in our society have no use for a smooth God, a smart God, an efficient, all-knowing, all-powerful God, who benignly congratulates our success and hard-won status, who knows the answers before we've stammered out the flicker of a question. In the face of the terrible experience of massive loss of faith, we now need a God of complexity, mutuality, empathy, and spontaneity, of blood and guts, of cancer and AIDS, of unexplained disease, of the abused and the abusing, of the homeless and those 'cared for by the community', of refugees and illegal immigrants, of those passed from one NHS department to another, of those who agonize about cloning and genetic modification, of those excluded from school again, of hopelessness, absent parents, and damaging relationships, of men without identity, and all whose eyes wander constantly to the full bottle of paracetamol.

In Chapter 1 I noted how frequently in mainstream Churches today we lay claim in language and strategy to being sacrament or agent of God's mission. One of my chief conversation-partners in asking 'What Church does God now invite us to become in the peculiarities of *this* time and *this* place?' is Jürgen Moltmann, who speaks constantly of God infecting the entire world with hope. This mission of hope is holistic. God's eschatological hope goes beyond predicting what will happen to us all in the end. Instead we are moved, together as a Church, to imagining the immense possibilities in the present moment of being already committed to working with God for God's final hope for all creation, 'the eschatological hope of justice, the humanising of man, the socialising of humanity, peace for all creation' (Moltmann, 1967, p. 329).

At the heart of Christian faith is God who is a community of difference, riskily open to the entire world in a polyphony of dynamic relationality.

This God is the fulcrum, the centre of gravity of the Christian under-standing of the self, the world and all reality. How would God have us rethink the deepest foundation for renovating the Church now? The identity and relevance of the Christian faith and of the community called to proclaim that faith cannot be separated. The cross of the risen Christ gives us the starting point required. Hope for the world flourishes in the memory of the future of Christ and also draws on the memory of Christ's death. In the risen Christ the unlimited potential of God's freedom is released into the world, through the Spirit in a diversity of ways. In the crucified Christ the shape of God's love for the liberation of all creation is revealed. Strategies for Church have a deep watermark already ingrained in the paper.

Instead of hastily drawing up efficient survival and entrepreneurial expansion schemes which assume that most people don't wish to think for themselves, Christ's Church will meditate on the irony of its vocation as a sign of the destiny of humanity and all creation to be renewed in the final coming together of all things in Christ. As we know from Christ, God's power is known in its opposite, the cross; and only in dying we can live. The Church that serves God's desire will bear the marks of Christ in its body. Basic in this regard is the thought of the new covenant that is intimately connected with the institution of the Eucharist and is also rooted in the understanding of the community of the Church as the shared, public life of the Body of Christ (1 Cor. 11.25–6). The hallmark of the character of God's mission is the cross, and the advance energy of this longing is the resurrection dispersed and made available by the energizing Spirit. So instead of being anxious about the authority and jurisdictional powers of ministers or the survival of Churches, we need to encourage deeper digging by everyone for the paradoxical foundations of a Church that could deal with the messy realities of plurality, diversity, contingency, the unreliability of a crucified God and of a world, the dynamic designs and reciprocal rhythms of which we have hardly begun to know.

A crucified God requires a Church that re-identifies its vocation again and again simultaneously in the light of the life and death of Jesus, the work of the Spirit now, the hope that God holds out to all creation, and the critical experiences and insights of our present context. In the remainder of this chapter I want to point to landmarks in contemporary thought that could be our partners in the present stage of the permanent and continuing task of renovating our ecclesial identity. My assumption is that we cannot adequately reconceive ourselves as Church simply from manipulating historic faith statements, however important and inspiring they may be. If God is God of all that exists a way forward could be through making contact with the many interweaving ways in which God is speaking to humanity now through dynamic patterns of conceiving the deep structure of reality: 'For God's identity does not rest on being outside but on *who* he is in *what* he does, on his being in his acts' (Hardy, 1996, p. 33).

Theories of connectedness

Theoretical concepts of field theories today increasingly allude to complex and fluid movements of interrelatedness, figure formation and destruction, and dynamic equilibrium. As the novelist Doctorow eloquently suggests, this language is overtaking the emphases of modernity on linear structure and individualism:

> The idea [is] that something can move in an absolute sense without reference to anything else. This is clearly impossible, a concept that cannot be proven. The ship that moves on the sea does so with reference to the land. Or if you prefer with reference to another ship, moving at a greater speed or a slower speed. Or by reference to a dirigible overhead. Or to a whale beneath the sea. Or to the currents of the sea itself. Always to something. There is nothing in the universe that can be proven to move absolutely without reference to something else in the universe, or for that matter without reference to the universe in its entirety.
>
> (E. L. Doctorow, 2000, p. 36)

I believe we need to work hard together now to discover attractive, integrated and workable theories and visions of Church to live in, struggle with, constantly test and improve. Those who are theologians and biblical students can work in partnership with the stimulus of those who work rigorously with different analogies, concepts, experiences and theories of the nature of the one reality that is God's creation. We need not fear to stand back, and through the lenses of a spectrum of disciplines, dare to open up the widest possible picture. God speaks to us certainly through the Bible, prayer, worship, theology and church community life. But God's truth has always been shown to us through people, relationships and human thought forms and patterns. Today for example, we can explore and critique the language and activities of social anthropologists who show us how to 'read' a complicated context – 'a community of consensual activities ruled and shaped by certain beliefs' (Patterson, 1999, p. 75) – and to understand better how human beings treat one another. God speaks also through physics and the newer passionate disciplines of psychotherapy.

My purpose here is to suggest the potential arising from intriguing and productive conversations between a number of revolutionary perceptions about reality and how parts interrelate that in some academic circles are proving to be very persuasive. This is not to blur the distinction between theology and quantum physics and sociobiology to create a fuzzy syncretism. Rather I would suggest that from many different areas of competence we hear the suggestion that the 'correspondence' view of reality, both in science and modern art, has broken down and that new paradigms require a cross-disciplinary approach (see Hardy, 1996, ch. 8). Reality cannot truly be perceived from a distance or understood as consisting of fragmented or in separate pieces, but as a participative and differentiated unity in which each one of us occupies our own unique and interrelated place. I want to express my excitement for the quest of finding a new basis for re-imagining the Church, of some awesome recent explorations of reality in terms of creative process, rather than as a collection of separate units.

Jesus the final scapegoat – René Girard

Asylum seekers and so-called illegal immigrants are currently high on the agenda of governments and media, as they compete on who can be harshest and toughest on unwanted people who should be excluded or locked up. In an increasingly global economy, hatred and the desire to control others is constantly triggered when the interests and sovereignty of those of us who are privileged are threatened. Closer to home, families often talk about having a 'black sheep' who has been shunned and excluded and denied her or his rightful place in the family constellation. For example, an alcoholic or drug-abusing parent might be demeaned, disrespected and eventually pushed out of a family, leaving young children without emotional access to them (as if they no longer existed and as if their situation had no connection whatsoever with the people and society around them). In communities when things go badly we look for the culprit and identify them as the sole cause of our distress. 'If only we had a different leader'; 'If only this team member would act like the rest of us'; 'If only she would use the Bible properly like me'; 'If only the administration would support us rather than attempt to remove our funding.' Such remarks suggest that René Girard's interdisciplinary insights on 'mimetic rivalry', conflict and the scapegoat offer a highly plausible resource to help us re-imagine a Church that checks itself from blaming individuals for the Church's experiences of failure, ridicule, and inadequacy.

I want to register the suggestive possibilities for creating a new atmosphere for re-conceiving the life of the Church today. His theory challenges the common practice in society and Church of finding victims to pay the price of shortcomings that in fact are the complex and common responsibility of entire communities, organizations and societies. Drawing together his reflections on texts in a collection of disciplines – psychology, sociology, politics and religion – Girard challenges widely accepted views of the autonomy of individuals to have aspirations. He suggests that in reality we borrow and give desires, aspirations and passions to one another. Tracing his theory through Greek tragedy (especially Sophocles' *Oedipus* and *Euripides*), philosophers (e.g. Derrida, Lacan, Levi-Strauss and Nietzsche), literature (e.g. the work of Dostoevsky and Cervantes) and Freud's work on the Oedipus complex, Girard concluded that 'mimesis' usually leads to a single victim becoming the focused recipient of collective violence (see Loughlin, 1997, p. 96ff.).

The term 'mimetic' or 'triangular' rivalry results from Girard's analysis of nineteenth-century literature. Our desires are imitated from models or mediators whose objects of desire become our objects of desire. But the model or mediator we copy can become our rival if we desire precisely the object he is imagined to have. Or other imitators of the same model may compete with us for the same objects. Jealousy and envy are inevitably aroused in such a mimetic situation. The romantic concept of a spontaneous desire is illusory, claims Girard (see Williams, 1996).

How common it is in Churches to elect a star, a mentor or role model, eagerly placing them on a pedestal because we admire them and would like some of what they've got or who they are. The passion we call 'hatred' arises when the very one we admire and whose life we desire to copy (as though without those qualities we ourselves are impotent), refuses to come up to our expectations or seemingly places obstacles in our way, leaving us as victims:

> Mere regret at not possessing something which belongs to another and which we covet is not enough to give rise to envy, since it might also be an incentive for acquiring the desired object or something similar ... *Envy* occurs only when our efforts to acquire it fail and we are left with a feeling of impotence.
>
> (Scheler in Williams, 1996, p. 41)

Girard's surrogate victim theory highlights how often in early myths and religious practices it was the sacrifice of the victim – 'unanimous immolation' by the whole community – that restored order from chaos or rescue from crisis. Humanity has a long history of protecting itself from nameless terrors by sacrificing one of our number and of defining who belongs in terms of who must be excluded. For example, the history of the delusion of the efficacy of scapegoating in European history includes accusations in the Middle Ages that Jews were responsible for the spread of plague. In his most influential work, *Things Hidden since the Foundation of the World* (1987), Girard subverts the agnostic intellectual world in his public espousal of Christ as the one through whom the operating of the scapegoat mechanism at last loses its hold.

An especially significant part of Girard's argument for a reflection on the diversification of Christian ministry is the recognition that any culture is a differential system, by which he means that it 'coheres as a unitary complex of differences and distinctions'. It is in denying the nature of complexity in which every person shares that some become marked as victim, a potential threat to the life of the system, often generating mob violence or their own exclusion. Recent history reveals increasingly gross acts of mob exclusion of those who spoil what would otherwise be perfect – ethnic cleansing in Bosnia, neo-Nazism in its various forms, Catholics and Protestants in Northern Ireland, paedophiles on British housing estates, catholics or liberals in the Church of England, bishops who do not conform to 'biblical' principles, or anyone whose beauty, wealth, power, sexuality, intelligence or lifestyle frightens us or stirs our envy. The belief in the efficacy of what Freud identifies as the collective murder of the guilty one, to bring resolution to the difficulty of the collective act of expulsion of the guilty one, has occupied a prominent place in Girard's explorations. Rather than having the desired result of finally resolving conflict, Girard suggests, mimetic rivalry violently escalates in a spiral of increased frustration. The practice of scapegoating would not hold credence as a way of reaching a peaceful settlement unless the community believed in the victim's counterbalancing capacity for creating evil.

After his studies of ancient world myths, Girard focused on the Judaeo-Christian texts further to explore the phenomenon of sacrificial elimination, only to find a radically different perspective because Israel's God is champion of the weak. The unique moral law of the Bible is that violence creates more violence. The 'founding murder' of Abel by Cain is not upheld but rejected as God sides with the victim and intervenes, 'Listen; your brother's blood is crying out to me from the ground!' (Gen. 4.10). Yet God places a mark on Cain as a guarantee of God's law against murder. So discord between doubles is succeeded by the order of the new community.

The Christ of the Gospels dies 'against sacrifice' but not as the victim of a vengeful God. He died at the hands of men and women that there might be no more sacrifice of victims. So there has to be a careful distinction from its use in other texts, if we are to avoid using the word 'sacrifice' as just retribution with reference to the death of Christ.

Girard advocates our consideration of the positive potential for more whole human relations if we were to allow the Judaeo-Christian understanding of sacrifice to act as a 'force of disruption' on habits of scapegoating informed by decadent mythologies. Girard encourages Christians to take with full seriousness the teaching of Jesus on the possibility of a Kingdom where enemies are loved and all are children of the Father. Human beings cannot avoid the act of mimetic rivalry it seems, but, at least theoretically, we are free to choose our models. In the parable of murderous vineyard tenants, Christ exposes and invites abandonment of the human chain of religions and cultures that define themselves by the rejection of the victim. Girard implores us to convert from or renounce the seductive power of imitation that produces and is generated by violence, and to take up the desire instead to follow Jesus and the Father through him. He is well aware of the fact that Jesus was crucified for daring to contradict the religious establishment and that, despite the action and example of Jesus, the Church for centuries has struggled, often unsuccessfully, with the old sacrificial systems of empire, hierarchy and control. He warns that we shall encounter violent resistance even today precisely when we attempt to reveal and to remove traditionally violent and excluding ways of creating community. Girard advocates the opening out of ourselves to others in love and the positive desire to imitate good in them. Here is the route to childlike love, creativity and community. He accepts as a basis for ethics the excessive desire on behalf of the Other, spoken of by the philosopher Edith Wyschorod; desiring for the other because of the otherness of the other, with empathy desiring for the other what the other desires for themself.

We should, I believe, be suspicious of any theory that elegantly claims to explain almost everything 'since the foundation of the world'. However, Girard makes an extremely significant contribution to helping us expose the violent dynamics that are the unconscious dominating factor in cultural orders. I would not want to push the case for his theories any further; however, tentatively and imaginatively I do want to place him in the web of those who can offer challenge and encouragement to the creative process of re-imagining the base of the Church's life and work.

I believe Girard's particular contribution is an example among many disciplines today of the recognition that a systemic approach recognizes that no one person is to blame, yet all of us carry our share of responsibility and of the opportunity to change the system (Neale, 2001, p. 7). I find this approach to be of great significance in the quest to find resources for reconfiguring church life, especially through the insights that:

- The God of Jesus Christ rejects the cultural mechanism of creating community through blaming and isolating individuals. The Church that sets out deliberately to make Jesus' life present here and now and to be an echo of trinitarian divine life will want to choose patterns of intimate relating with God and all people as a significant element of its character and task. Ford in *Self and Salvation* evocatively develops this notion in terms of transformational communities of facing (see Ford, 1999, pp. 17–29, 170ff.).

- However uncomfortable for us, the evidence is that marginalizing people is not the sin of a few highly politicized and especially devious individuals. Some people may be able to manipulate these processes to their own ends (as the crowds who had welcomed him as he entered Jerusalem were persuaded to shout for the death of Jesus, not Barabbas), but mimetic desire and rivalry is a collective phenomenon in which everyone routinely participates.

- It is extremely difficult to persuade people of the reality of scapegoating because it is so uncomfortable to bear. I can feel a definite sense of excitement in contemplating what it would be like for a Church to dare to define itself and for Christians to practise relating, in ways that do not define who belongs by who is pushed to the edge, ignored or excluded.

- Trying to beat our rivals at their own game with a drive to be top of the hierarchy of dominance is a feature of all community life. It is hard to know ourselves as scapegoaters and equally hard to be personally honest about the lengths to which we will go to walk over others to be first. Apart from violent urges that probably lie deep within our biology, there are clearly soul and spiritual issues here. This is about more than individual discipline and concerns the continuum of mimesis affecting the model and character of the church community.

- Church processions and liturgies are acted-out scenes of mimesis. Among all the courtesies and gentleness of entering, marking out and occupying the sacred space strides both the crude if unconscious desire to exclude and to be noticed as important. This is not a private game for public ministers but becomes unanimous, affecting the entire community.

- As the history of monarchs reveals, communities love to crown kings as gods for a time. They have within them their own victim destiny so that their times of unpopularity, dethroning and execution are part of the whole scenario. Churches and their leaders play on this victim theme, occasionally coming to the crisis of exclusion to save or redefine the whole Church. But it doesn't have to be so.

- If a Church, unaware of its mimetic rivalry patterns, senses that it is disintegrating and losing its energy and influence, it must seek a cause in society outside itself. It cannot easily dare to know and face its own self-destructive forces. We need a deep courage not constantly to name new scapegoats for our Church's sense of lostness and usefulness – television, Sunday sport and trading, lack of support for all organizations today, or new patterns of employment and leisure.

Wholeness as a flowing movement – quantum field theory

'Quantum field theory', invented by Paul Dirac in the late 1920s, points to a previously unknown 'togetherness in separation' in the fabric of the universe (Polkinghorne, 1990). The physicist David Bohm, now widely recognized for his significant contributions to the discussion on the relationship between art and science, has committed himself to reducing confusion in relating theories to reality. Some may react to my electing to dialogue with Bohm, claiming that his 'spirituality' is of a suffused and general nature and hardly relevant to reviewing the Church's ministry. But if our Christian framework includes nothing less than the whole of God's life in the whole of reality, provided we allow for the testing of the Spirit, we need not be afraid of experimenting with new language, looking at reality through the lens of concepts not originating in the Christian tradition in the task of discovering adequate-enough images for the Church to inhabit. The ideas of Church we choose and the experiences of Church we have and help to create work on each other constantly and cannot finally be separated or defined. Bohm points to the gradual recognition that scientific theories do not reflect an objectively certifiable world. He uses the expression 'experience-knowledge' crucially to argue that our theories are not true copies of 'reality as it is', but constantly shifting forms of insight, giving temporary shape and form to experience.

His work on the self-organizing quality of reality, leading him to a belief in the unending limitation of all theories to describe 'reality as it is', has a particular reference to our patterns of defining experience in terms of the fragmentation or separation of parts of reality. At a practical level Newtonian theory often has value in listing or separating distinct (large and slowly moving) elements to understand them better but, argues Bohm, we must not fall into the illusion of believing that the world is actually constituted of separate parts and therefore proceed to act in such a way as to produce fragmentation in what is in fact whole. Bohm encourages us to resist any kind of Olympian, integrated overview or imposed unity as this itself would be merely a form of fragmentation. Our primary reality, he suggests, is an unbroken wholeness or implicate order. 'Rather, all our different ways of thinking are to be considered as different ways of looking at the one reality, each with some domain in which it is clear and adequate' (Bohm, 1995, pp. 7f.).

He compares a theory to a particular, and limited, view of some object. It requires an immense range of views to begin to perceive the reality in its entirety, but the reality itself is not to be thought of in the fragments of our ways of seeing, but rather as a holographic picture, a massive, restless energy flow. So Bohm invites us to move beyond the view of classical atomic theory that, except in some limited situations, each particle has meaning and that an observer can take a neutral position or have a separate existence from that which is observed. Quantum theory has shown that observer and observed merge and interpenetrate in a whole and indivisible reality. To get the truest impression of the universal flux of events, processes, movement and energy, Bohm imagines that each particle has a field extending through space and merging with the fields of other particles. He illustrates his proposal for a new general form of insight with the idea of 'undivided wholeness in flowing movement' in which thoughts and ideas, with differing degrees of permanence and stability, move as ripples, waves and vortices in a stream of consciousness. So he conceives of matter as an undivided whole in flowing movement within which various patterns have limited autonomy and stability.

His complex and subtle account of the universe, implied in some modern developments in physics, emphasizes that nothing is to be understood as independent or permanently existing but instead as a product that has been formed for a while in the flowing movement and that will ultimately dissolve back into this movement. Each particle forms and maintains its existence according to its particular place and function in the whole:

> Parts are seen to be in immediate connection, in which their dynamical relationships depend, in an irreducible way, on the whole system (and indeed, on that of broader systems in which they are contained, extended ultimately and in principle to the entire universe). Thus, one is led to a new notion of *unbroken wholeness* which denies the classical idea of analysability of the universe into separately independently existent parts.
>
> (Zukav, 1979, p. 312)

Bohm is frustrated that an atomistic view of particles and a generally fragmentary view of reality, against overwhelming evidence, continue to dominate the discipline of physics. The responsive relationship between ideas and actions means that holding the view that the world can be understood as separate units, beyond the realm in which to do so is appropriate, is effectively an attempt to divide what cannot be divided. World views rooted in such fragmentation can have disastrous social, political, economical, ecological and psychological effects.

In discovering more effective ways of being Church to serve God's saving purpose *(missio Dei)* in all the world, we can be assisted by giving careful attention to Bohm's emphasis on the subtle and difficult nature of understanding wholeness and fragmentation. As we meditate on the future of Christian community living, I find it vital to be aware that the content of theories, which can never exist separately from thinking processes, are merely ways of addressing problems or, like poetry, not capable of being direct equations with things as they really are. As a reflective strategist in the Church I find myself resonating with Bohm's belief that the art form of theorizing about reality as one implicate order requires discernment to know which aspects should properly change slowly and which rapidly. Certainly mistakes occur when we fail to start with the whole, encapsulated completely in each part, and when we neglect to see ourselves there within the fluctuating process of knowledge. A Church which claims to be a sign or foretaste of God's coming ordering of the cosmos must have difficulty when its choice of self-ordering among its members and leaders is frequently a portrayal of isolationism, adversarial competition for superiority and control:

> We need to let go of the monotheistic, patriarchal dogmas of our recent past. No matter how well they may have served us, they are no longer appropriate or adequate for the emerging world of our time. The holistic consciousness, engaging the will and imagination of increasing numbers of people, calls us to new ways of being in the world, not in oppositional isolation or confrontation, but in convivial co-operation with our evolving universe leading us to fresh horizons of wholeness (holiness), hope, and possibility.
>
> (O'Murchu, 1997, pp. 60f.)

In 1964 John S. Bell, an Irish physicist working at the European Organization for Nuclear Research in Switzerland, published a deeply significant mathematical theorem intimately connecting the separate parts of the universe. He contends that a correlation can exist between what happens, at a single moment of time, to objects some distance from each other. Bell challenges the common-sense understanding of reality in everyday use as unable to describe subatomic phenomena or even many aspects of everyday living (Sharpe, 2000). Like Bohm, Bell admits that classical fragmentary modes of thought may sometimes be a practical tool for dealing with the world but should not be regarded as trustworthy as a description of 'that-which-is'.

Quantum theory has shown that togetherness in separation is a key characteristic of the natural world and that even subatomic entities cannot be treated atomistically (Layzer, 1990; Polkinghorne, 1990). I wish to argue that because the dynamic and innovative character of Christian thought and practice means that it is always renewing itself in fresh and amazing ways ('repenting'), Christianity has the resilience to dialogue with scientists in many branches of learning who are engaged in the creation of a radically new language to describe the exuberance and complex possibilities in the world's activity. This process of rippling out to find new, deep patterns of relating in church communities is an example of the Holy Spirit leading us into all truth (John 16.12–15). In particular the Western Church's preoccupation with independence and separation as a way of describing itself could respond to the challenge of modern scientific theories that mutual interdependence and paradox are vital keys to the identity of all life and growth. Failure to allow the deep insights of contemporary science to have an impact on the Church's awareness and consciousness can surely only further seal our fate as deliberately becoming further alienated from God and humanity.

Everything affects everything – Gestalt theory

Gary M. Yontef, Gestalt therapist and theorist, explores another aspect of this process of conceiving wholeness in terms of dynamic inter-relatedness. *Awareness, Dialogue and Process* (1993) documents more than 20 years of Yontef's writing and thinking on the theory of Gestalt therapy. Aligning himself with those twentieth-century physicists who have moved on from classical theories of objective observation and logical predictability, he describes all reality in terms of contact and changing process. Yontef describes the revolutionary approach of Gestalt therapists, such as Fritz Perls and James Simkin, as engaging with the what and how of a person's process in the present moment. I have neither the intention nor the skill to summarize Gestalt theory but will attempt briefly to draw out for our purposes here the particular contribution to seeing things whole that is so characteristic of this therapy framework.

Yontef defines all reality primarily as 'relating' in that people grow in their contact with the environment: 'We grow by what happens between people, not by looking inward' (Yontef, 1993, p. 33). He defines the person or self in terms of the interrelations between the person and the rest of the dynamic whole or field. With clear echoes of Bohm and Bell, he reminds us that there is *no* behaviour that is definable except as a function of the field. All behaviour is a function of the field:

The complex system of contacts necessary for adjustment in the difficult field, we call 'self'. Self may be regarded as at the boundary of the organism, but the boundary is not itself isolated from the environment; it contacts the environment; it belongs to both, environment and organism.

(Perls, Hefferline and Goodman, in Yontef, 1993, p. 33)

The language and definition that is most relevant to our enquiry into how to study and imagine a system and its operation concerns field theory, though strictly speaking there are numerous 'field theories'. Notably, Koffka writes:

It has become apparent that the true solution ... cannot be a machine theory based on a sum of independent sensory processes, but must be a thoroughly dynamic theory in which the processes organize themselves under the prevailing dynamic and constraining conditions.

(Latner, 1983, p. 75)

In Yontef's summary, formally defined field theories assume that:

• a field is a dynamic framework for understanding elements of reality as a set of mutually influencing and even conflicting forces, a systemic web of relationships;
• a field is continuous in space and time, a unified, interactive whole field, an organized whole, not the unity of essentially separate aspects and not a linear or historical sequence;
• the identity of every object, event or organism can only be known as of-a-field, intrinsically effecting and affected by the field;
• so phenomena are determined by the entire field in mutual interaction;
• the field is a unitary whole of processes and events, including observer and observed: everything affects everything else in the field.

A growing body of literature reveals clusters of unresolved controversy about varying models and definitions. The leading attitude within Gestalt therapy is the radically different way of being aware known as 'field theory', which enables dynamic organizing concepts – such as contact, figure and ground, boundary and the self as a creative process – to exist. 'It is the cognitive glue that holds the Gestalt therapy system together' (Yontef, 1993, p. 324). As such, and from the inevitably superficial understanding of anyone who has not trained or practised as a Gestalt therapist, I tentatively suggest it has great potential for encouraging the Church to let go of its Newtonian views of polarized and linear cause and effect, and dare to conceive itself and therefore to act as though every part is really contributing to the entire web of relationships. This is unlikely to be immediately accepted by most people as the 'false dichotomies' with which 'the road to hell is paved' (David Jenkins) have served our Church well enough for so long.

In my own experience of family, community and church life, field theory certainly makes connections. In the field of a diocese there will be clergy who usually resort to the history of the last 40 years as a way of explaining everything; laity who need a regular 'fix' from the neighbourhood Church of a different tradition from their regular one; clergy who take on the role of subverting any tendencies towards getting too serious about faith; those whose primary interest lies in the minutiae of hagiography or in another part of the globe and so many more – all part of the field – all holding a particular polarity. Sometimes when I become eloquent on the subject of the Trinity, I notice from the response in others that I too am holding some important insights for the community – and equally need to hear with high attention those that others are holding. But I know from my own experience how far it can be from the head to the body. I can know that unless I acknowledge my negative as well as positive feelings, I shall suffer more headaches or experience regular exhaustion. Yet in a church culture that speaks eloquently of the passion of Christ in both his living and dying, I can still find constraints to expressing the feelings that I am experiencing or in expecting others to do so. Even with so many women now enlarging the field of possibilities in the Church, I notice how intrusive the mention of anger, fear or sadness can be. For me it is a persistent process to move through, gradually changing my perceptions of how reality is structured to practising awareness, speech, behaviour and relating that are consistent with this new approach.

Combining solutions for global problems – Freeman J. Dyson

The search for eco- or geo-justice claims our moral attention as we recognize that the dignity and freedom of humanity cannot be separated from the present and future health of our planetary home (see O'Murchu, 1997 and Moltmann, 1989a). The vocation of the Church is explored in the wide canvas of a world where an urgent agenda includes unity between peoples in the service of a common good and the desire for an interwoven texture of peoples with the natural world as an expression of unity with God.

Freeman Dyson, physicist and interpreter of scientific discovery, has spent a lifetime exploring how scientific designs can be tools for improving the quality of human life on the planet. He is passionate about the new possibilities that emerge when clusters of disciplines and issues are brought together, holistically, displacing the assumption, for example, that technology separate from politics, religion, economics and military and cultural issues can solve a problem. For example, he has used the laws of physics to try to build a safer form of nuclear reactor, and has connected applied mathematics with reducing the killing and maiming power of landmines in Cambodia, Bosnia, Angola and Afghanistan.

Dyson's concern is to have a world that is not driven by one concern or set of energies to the detriment of others. He proposes, for example, that the evil of rural poverty can be tackled through a holistic harnessing of technology and ethics together. He points to Mexico City as one of the ten megacities in the world with populations twice as large as New York. Migration to such cities has a cluster of causes including massive population increases, unemployment and poverty in the countryside. Dyson proposes that the miseries of the entire situation could be reduced through a combination of solar energy, genetic engineering and the Internet. He believes that a halt to rising poverty would probably decelerate the population growth.

Dyson personally witnessed and studied the collapse of the East German economy after the communist period. In his analysis, the reasons for the wrecking of the rural economy included the phenomena that Russia would no longer buy from the farmers because the price had to be paid in West German marks; that German customers found the products to be of poorer quality than was available in supermarkets; and that French and Danish products were being imported. The results, generally replicated in villages throughout the world, were that East German farmers felt it was no longer worthwhile to continue; young people unable to find work moved away from the villages to the cities; old and young remaining in the rural communities are mostly unemployed and reduced to poverty; and the local zoo – established and subsidized in the communist era, a source of local pride and security – had to be closed.

Dyson describes the slow and steady revival taking place in the rural economy of East Germany with these elements: the arrival of new people with money; these new wealthy residents buy and modernize local buildings; some of the old farming families move out; native villagers have been offered low-interest government loans to buy modern houses; farming co-operatives have been offered low-interest government loans to modernize; old cottages have been combined to create larger houses with double garages; some of the old families are sharing in the new prosperity; the zoo has been reopened; a new vineyard has been established; many who live there commute to work in the cities; the roads have been widened and modernized to make room for larger vehicles; the ancient church has been repaired and restored; and the concerns of ecologists are being given priority in nearby forests and mountains, so there is now a sense of achievement and happiness.

As I read Dyson's account of the situation in East Germany, it was occurring to me how often I have observed a similar pattern in parts of Yorkshire, the Cotswolds, Essex, and Wales, where I have lived and worked in recent years. Features of changes in Britain and France include: fewer residents involved in farming; property and amenity improvements and a sense of prosperity associated with new, wealthy residents; nostalgia promoting the revival of old crafts and buildings; increasing meeting of the needs of tourism; and a better-paid local population with a sense of security. Change in one part of a context inevitably means change in every part. Dyson, noting how rural revival has come not from one source but from a cluster, asks how this could become a reality to halt the flow of people from villages to megacities throughout the world, with the consequent poverty and degradation.

Dyson gives an account of how the Solar Electric Light Fund (SELF) – whose director, Bob Freling, is fluent in Spanish, Russian, French, Chinese, Portuguese, and Indonesian – operates small companies to generate electricity by sunlight in a variety of remote parts of the world. Some of the advantages of a working, solar-energy system in a remote village are: a 30 or 40 watt input can run two fluorescent lights, a radio or a small black-and-white television for several hours; each hut can have its own system; there is no need for a central generator, cables or transformers; sunlight is distributed equally to each roof top; children can read and study at home in the evening; and the village can make contact with the rest of the world.

The SELF organization is charitably based, and gives credit over four years for villagers to buy the lightweight but strong equipment. It has paid for the necessary training, installation, operating and maintenance of the hardware in village projects in 11 countries. When the technology for the global Internet to reach these remote villages is achievable, they will have access to the Internet. The technology to enable the use of sunlight to generate electricity is still expensive and small-scale, requiring more research. The traditional harnessing of the sun to grow crops for food and trees for fuel presents problems when forests are fast disappearing. From the existence of so much solar energy on the earth, Dyson argues that technology has to be found to make it less expensive. He looks to the development of a technology that combines photo-electric and biological systems in ways that I need not describe here in detail. The result could be a supply of solar energy that is cheap, plentiful and environmentally sensitive.

His hopes for a radical decrease in the cost and increase of efficiency in energy crops rest on the genome. Dyson suggests that genetic engineering will transform energy supplies in the future in a combination of: attractive landscaping; variations of tree species; sensitivity to human settlement and wildlife; attractive financial incentives for tree growers; and capitalizing on people's attraction to having trees in their close environment:

> Cheap solar energy and genetic engineering will provide the basis for primary industries in the countryside, modernised farming and mining and manufacturing. After that, the vast variety of secondary and tertiary economic activities that use the internet for their co-ordination, food processing and publishing and education and entertainment and health care, will follow the primary industries as they move away from overgrown cities to country towns and villages. As soon as the villages become rich, they will attract people and wealth back from the cities.
>
> (Dyson, 1999, p. 73)

Of course not everyone wants to live in villages and there are plenty of questions about what happens when you've got a 'rich village', but I include Dyson in this brief survey of theories of wholeness because of his passionate holistic approach to discovering ways to human flourishing. David Bohm has shown that the notion that the world and our universe are made up of separate 'things' is an illusion and leads to endless confusion. He explains the work of the Belgian chemist, Ilya Prigogine, in a way that resonates with the practical application of Dyson. Studying the emergence and development of life, Prigogine proposes that self-organization may be a fundamental law of science:

> His work demonstrated the capacity for certain chemical systems – he named them 'dissipative structures' – to regenerate to higher levels of self-organisation in response to environmental demands. Such emergent properties have been found across a wide variety of domains. In addition to oscillating chemical reactions, they've been found in fluid vortices, lasers, genetic networks, immune networks, neural networks, and ecosystems, as well as in social systems. All of these diverse phenomena have one thing in common: in each case a network of interacting elements gives rise to the emergence of a new entity with completely new properties. If you try to pinpoint the 'conductor', it is nowhere to be found. You cannot pinpoint it.
>
> (Jaworski, 1998, p. 176; and see Sharpe, 2000, pp. 8ff.)

Dyson's combination of ethics, scientific theory, technological adventure, financial realism, psychology and sheer flair for encouraging a flow of energy in the hope of a better world seems to me an attractive echo of the diverse and holistic energy needed in re-imagining the Church. Indeed the Local Ministry movement, to which I shall be referring later, contains the seeds to create local missionary Christian communities that listen to and transform their contexts and are themselves changed and enriched in the process.

The underlying order in Dyson's explorations of human flourishing in relation with creation resonates with a trinitarian belief in God. God is no mere observer from the outside and God does not intervene to deprive human beings of their responsibility but energizes people to work in companionship with all to 'allow all sorts of creatures a fair chance of a life of their own choosing' (S. Clark, in Page, 2000, p. 182). Responding in faith to the triune God of complexly ordered energy gives us confidence in the future. Yet the absence of control at the heart of this contingent ordering and the human freedom of response leave the future hopeful but always unresolved.

Total self-definition – Timothy Jenkins

At an Edward King Institute consultation on Local Ministry at Leicester in 1988, Timothy Jenkins demonstrated how for social anthropologists the phenomena that constitute a locality must be read in ways that go beyond imposed interpretation, statistics and feelings. There can be no detached observer. In his essay, 'Faith Embedded in the Particularities of History', Daniel W. Hardy describes how Aleksandr Solzhenitsyn employs the notion of 'knots' or critical moments in history, developing in his novels 'concentrated and minutely detailed accounts of events within strictly limited periods of time, with complete breaks between them' (Hardy, 1996, pp. 261ff.). From such narrative:

> The larger task for historical theology is that of identifying the dynamic by which the most concentrated forms of human life in the world – rationality, society and culture interacting with nature – exemplify the work of God in the world. For this, existing views of these forms of human life and of the work of God in the world are unlikely to suffice, since they are both static and self-contained. What will be required is understandings of rationality, society and culture – and God's work in them – which are both conditional and contingent upon their future.
>
> (Hardy, 1996, p. 278)

Another social anthropologist, Joy Hendry, makes the link with the Heisenberg uncertainty principle, which recognized the need to introduce a change to particles of reality to observe them: 'Anthropologists can learn from and about their own experience in the process of understanding people elsewhere' (Hendry, 1999, p. 28).

Believing that our humanness is acquired and shaped in particular experiences of community, Jenkins' challenge to the study of religion in communities in Britain abandons an objective method that labels and compartmentalizes from a point of either separation or superiority. Jenkins explores religion as part of the elision of phenomena (of processes of knowing and acting, on equal terms with content) that in their combinations create communities and institutions. His time-consuming personal sharing in the experiences of a Whit Walk in Bristol and of a rural village near Cambridge leads to his insight that attempts to describe religious behaviour as separate from the assumptions, conversation and practices of the whole of life will be incomplete. Subverting the tendency today to isolate committed church membership from everyday issues of human flourishing, Jenkins, the ethnographer, seems to go to the opposite extreme of neglecting to recognize and celebrate the particular energy and shape of Christian worship and living. However, his insights that we are inseparable from our stories and that the religious dimension of human flourishing cannot properly be extricated from everyday living offer further examples of a contemporary theory of connectedness.

Nicholas Healy affirms the value of ethnographic descriptions, showing 'how ideas, events and institutions interact and change through time', an approach sometimes called 'processual analysis': 'To describe adequately any given social pattern we cannot simply describe its present form, but must acknowledge the process by which it arrives at that form' (Healy, 2000, p. 180).

Jenkins questions the familiar analysis of the religious dimension to community life that takes as opposites religion and modernity, success and decline, public and private, and emotion and intellect. His approach, which he puts forward with no certain assumption of its fruitfulness, is a social anthropology or a careful description of everyday happenings in particular localities together with a process for testing their various contested interpretations.

Social anthropology concerns itself with the interplay of hidden and disclosed elements in the annual parade through Kingswood. Jenkins writes, 'Thought, actions and interpretation together form a complex simultaneity' – the combination of church leaders and notable citizens, families, organizations, participants and watchers, the ordering of the route. Social anthropologists note how, in society generally, without claiming to know everything, we make some sense of what we see and of how we are ourselves participants rather than disinterested observers. Jenkins draws two conclusions from his giving attention to the interacting phenomena of participants and spectators, statements of intent and ways of defining meaning:

- Communities define themselves and find cohesion through the total interaction of occupying a particular space, over a period of time, with laws that arise from within that social grouping.
- The self-definition of the social group is complex, but continually built up through ways of behaving, belonging and negotiating status. These find expression through family, place of residence and employment, as well as through involvement in local voluntary organizations, and the development of singular personal qualities.

So that overall, Jenkins can say of the Whit Walk:

> The procession is a particularly complete moment in which the procedures of claim and negotiation that make up a whole way of life are made clear: it is a moment of public accounting, both with respect to the outside gaze and with respect to the infinite calculations of internal differences.
>
> (Jenkins, 1999a, p. 8)

I believe we can see very fluid connections here with quantum theory and Gestalt theory and the other examples of challenge to compartmentalized, fragmented, and individualistic frames of reference still so prevalent in scholarly debate (Douglas, 1994). Jenkins deduces from the disciplined paying attention of fieldwork that *both* inquirer and the objects of the inquiry are bound up in the local process, and 'this includes making sense of the other' (Jenkins, 1999a, p. 11).

There is no possibility of being a detached observer. There are two further consequences. The first is that particular communities of persons are principally an ordering of the different phenomena of force, constraint and obligation. The second is that events, relationships and social contracts on differing scales 'are all products of the complex interplay of potentials and incapacities, claims and concealments, belongings-to and exclusions from, becomings and annihilations, that constitute the expressions of motivations' (Jenkins, 1999a, p. 11).

So I believe these insights from social anthropology add weight to cumulative argument of this chapter that no thing or person can truly exist or be interpreted as alone, but only as part of a web of negotiations and interplay of personalities, obligations and interplay of mutual interpretations of what is taking place here and now.

The triune God: mystery of relation – Elizabeth Johnson

The Christian tradition has its own lively contribution to seeing things whole, rooted in centuries of reflection on and worship of the triune God who is a community of difference. As Alan J. Torrance suggests:

> If subatomic physics has disposed of the myth that at the most basic level we must posit some primordial substance to be conceived as the ground and postulate of the notion of relations, trinitarian theology has (analogically!) suggested precisely this at the theological and cosmological levels!
>
> (Torrance, 1996, p. 258)

Some of the leading theologians of recent decades, beginning notably with Karl Barth, have presented us with overlapping concepts and terminology in their attempts to speak of a doctrine of the triune God which takes seriously the mutuality of loving communion experienced in the community of the Church, opened up for us in the person and work of Christ by the Spirit:

> The communion of the Trinity as such constitutes the *arche* and *telos* of all that is. It provides the hermeneutical criterion of all that has existence (of good as well as evil) and compels us to conceive and reinterpret Being in terms of divine personhood and the ultimacy of the intra-divine personal communion. That the critical controls on the understanding of this would have to remain radically theological (and therefore *a posteriori*) and not anthropological is expressed in Barth's emphatic reminder, 'This is the unique divine trinity, in the unique divine unity'. Nothing less, therefore, than the most fundamental ontological and cosmological issues are at stake here in the debate concerning the mutuality and communion which characterises the Trinity.
>
> (Torrance, 1996, pp. 258f.)

Colin Gunton, David Ford and Alan Torrance are among the prominent British exponents of a reappraisal of the importance of a trinitarian knowledge of God as an imaginative resource for moving the Church out of the polarization between liberal and conservative positions. I have chosen Elizabeth Johnson's particular reading of this because she offers an incisive exploration of the ontology of triune personhood, specifically anchoring her vision of God in the vivifying ways of the Spirit, the compassionate, liberating story of Jesus, the generative mystery of the Creator, all co-creating the inexhaustible mystery of the multifaceted experience of the one God:

> *beyond, with and within*
> *behind, with and ahead*
> *above, alongside and around us.*
> (Johnson, 1998, p. 191)

The Christian experience, from New Testament times until now, of being met in this diversity of saving ways suggests that God's own being as communion is somehow similarly differentiated, 'a dynamic coming and going with the world, which points to an inner divine circling around in unimaginable relation. Not an isolated, static, ruling monarch but a relational, dynamic, tripersonal mystery of love' (Johnson, 1998, p. 192).

Johnson shows how in recent centuries the doctrine of Trinity has run into a cluster of problems that have reduced the attraction of trinitarian speech about God. In part this is due to the separation of the doctrine from actual multifaceted experiences of God's love. So it becomes a cerebral theory apparently referring to God literally, in terms of a mathematical calculation or as reinforcing hierarchical patterns of subordination. Feminists have struggled with trinitarian imagery, which is predominantly and uncritically suggesting that men only, a fraternity, rather than men and women together reveal the essence of God.

The possible value for the argument of this chapter emerges when Johnson pioneers new possibilities for expressing the ancient truth about God that is still compelling through the use of nonpersonal terms such as Abba, servant, Paraclete, and retrieving a nonpatriarchal meaning of Father of Jesus Christ. Catherine Mowry LaCugna takes a similar approach to the revitalization of a trinitarian conceiving of God's self-expressive and giving life in the opposing of every kind of subordination between persons and 'everything that deceives us into believing self-aggrandising archaisms' (LaCugna, 1991, p. 401). Johnson works to find metaphors for the profound Christian experience of God as an equal, mutual, reciprocal dynamism of communion. She commends Jürgen Moltmann's exploration of how Scripture makes it possible to conceive of the trinitarian persons in different patterns of relation from a set of linear progressions. Moltmann argues rightly that 'The unity of God is to be found in the triunity of the Father, the Son and the Holy Spirit. It neither precedes nor follows it' (Moltmann, 1989b, p. 190). The three persons of God interweave each other in various patterns of saving activity and can be spoken about in concepts such as giving over receiving back, being obedient, being glorified, witnessing, filling and actively glorifying.

This is in contrast with inherited models of God and Church that assume that unless a single ruler is controlling everyone from above, chaos will emerge, personal identity will become blurred and harmony be lost. Johnson recalls with passion the warnings of feminist thinkers from Virginia Woolf to Mary Daly to 'beware the processions of educated men' (Johnson, 1998, p. 197).

Johnson urges us to abandon literalness in using symbols, remembering that this dense symbol of God's mystery arises from historical experiences of Jews and later Gentiles, through Jesus in the Spirit's power, experiencing salvation. Referring to Karl Rahner, she asks us to keep in mind that trinitarian language can only ever serve as an analogy, reflecting on experience, 'speculation can degenerate into wild and empty conceptual acrobatics' (Johnson, 1998, p. 198). Rather than being an attempt at a literal description, the trinitarian symbol has the ability to convey the fundamental experience of *shalom* drawing near. Trinity is shorthand for the inexpressible dynamic in which the Sophia-God of compassionate, liberating love comes to each person and situation in uniquely different ways.

So, supported by Karl Rahner and Piet Schoonenberg, Johnson invites us today to rediscover the possibilities of trinitarian concepts by lifting up the threefold experience of the mystery of God as the point of departure for understanding. Although all our words are opaque, trinitarian language is a pointer to the belief that God's plan for redemption, shown in Jesus Christ and the work of the Spirit, reveals no less than God in God's true self. Our faith is that the liberation we know is the passionate livingness of Godself in and for the world. As LaCugna writes, 'In knowing the God who is our origin, ground, goal, we do not know a shadow of God but the real living God of Jesus Christ in the Spirit. The God who saves – this is God' (Johnson, 1998, p. 201).

To say 'Trinity' is to use an analogy of divine livingness, to express belief in God who is like a threefoldness of relation. In the context of this chapter, the symbol of Trinity, as avidly discussed by Johnson and others I have mentioned, opens up three avenues for further reflection.

- The symbol of Trinity expresses that the very essence of the God – at the heart of all reality and shown to us particularly in the dynamic of Christian community and the Eucharist – is relatedness, rather than solitary ego.
- This symbol indicates that the particular kind of relatedness than which nothing greater can be conceived is not one of hierarchy

involving domination and subordination, but rather one of genuine mutuality in which there is radical equality, while distinctions are respected.

- The trinitarian God, moreover, cannot be spoken about without reference to a divine outpouring of compassionate, liberating love in the historical world of beauty, sin, suffering, so leading to the envisioning of God empowering human praxis along the same patterns.

I believe we can draw on the powerful affinity between the analogy of God as a community of simultaneous and participative meeting of persons, with much contemporary awareness of relationality as a way of being in the world as we have encountered it already in the pages above. The implications are great for reconceiving Church in which each person is constituted by their relationships to each other and each is unintelligible except as connected with the others, and no statement about one is true if taken in isolation from the other.

As relations equally constitute God's being, there is no absolute divine person – there are only the relative three. At the heart of holy mystery is not monarchy but community; not an absolute ruler but a threefold *koinonia*. Johnson, with reference to familiar stories of Jesus and the disciples, suggests that this relatedness could be experienced and expressed as genuine friendship in all its freedom to relate across social barriers, trusting the reliability of others in genuine reciprocal regard. Such friends can walk side by side in common interests, sharing common delights, taking up shared responsibilities, including others in the circle, which is an essential stance of hospitality. She is using friendship here not in the collusive sense of overlapping, undifferentiated sameness, but rather friendship as constituted by personal distinctiveness.

The metaphor of God as a Trinity of friendship can be spun out in terms of the essential relating at the heart of the mystery of reality, humanity and the world, the different nations and cultures interrelating, the search for peace and justice, the uniqueness of each human being, and a Church of rich, complex differentiated unity.

Finally, I find a deep resonance with the Gospel accounts of the intimate relationships and mutual dialogue between Spirit, Father and Son in the way that Johnson takes up Edmund Hill's reflections on the Greek *perichoresis*. She draws a word picture of the two-way vitality intrinsic to God's triunity, modelled on the rhythmic, simultaneous ebb and flow of a country-folk, round dance as one way to portray the mutual indwelling, energetic congruence and encircling of God's holy mystery. She suggests taking this further to portray the anguish and ecstasy of the contemporary spirit:

Dancers whirl and intertwine in unusual patterns; the floor is circled in seemingly chaotic ways; rhythms are diverse; at times all hell breaks loose; resolution is achieved unexpectedly. Music, light and shadow, colour, and wonderfully supple motion coalesce in dancing that is not smoothly predictable and repetitive, as is a round dance, and yet it is just as highly disciplined. Its order is more complex. Casting the metaphor in yet another direction, we can say that the eternal flow is stepped to the contagious rhythm of spicy salsas, meringues, calypsos, or reggaes where dancers in free motion are yet bonded in the music. Perichoretic movement summons up the idea of all three distinct persons existing in each other in an exuberant movement of equal relations: an excellent model for human inter-action in freedom and other regards. Precisely as community in diversity Holy Wisdom has the capacity to be the ground of the turning world.

(Johnson, 1998, p. 221; and see Boff, 1992, pp. 137ff.)

The continuing ecumenical debate on trinitarian communion at the heart of God invites us to take an integrative, dynamic of participation as the major clue to all our explorations of the proper nature of human personhood, baptism, church community, Eucharist, worship and Christian ministry. We are given these as provisional signs of the new creation that the triune life of God will bring about in the end.

Interfaith prayer – Gavin D'Costa

Clearly writing as a Roman Catholic, but one deeply influenced by theologians of other traditions, D'Costa offers a framework for asking the question whether prayer with people of other faiths can be consistent with faithfulness to his tradition. I am deliberately introducing D'Costa's work here because he begins from a perichoretic trinitarian understand-ing of Christian prayer and the whole of life.

He argues that such prayer, rather than an act of faithlessness, could be experienced and known as a way of knowing more fully the life of the triune God through the Spirit at work in other religions. D'Costa starts out from the intense relationship with God of Thérèse de Lisieux that led her to regard prayer as part of our communal love affair with God in all the conditions of human living. Further, she came to see that participat-ing in trinitarian love is to 'make a loan' from this love and to share in this 'unique source' (D'Costa, 2000, p. 145).

D'Costa shows awareness of the degree of scandal caused among British Churches by public acts of prayer with communities of other faiths who do not believe the Christian faith or worship God as Trinity.

The level of hurt is shown, for example, by an open letter publicly signed by 70 key church persons and a further 2,000 supporters in October 1991. Further exploration shows that the sharp issue for the signatories was behaviour that seemed to challenge the uniqueness of Christianity for salvation. On the international level, Pope John Paul II's initiative for a day of prayer for peace at Assisi in 1986 is just one example of many events, each of which varies in significance depending on such factors as venue, intention, gender and status of participants, and other issues such as degree of representative authorization.

Taking the orthodoxy of the Roman Catholic catechism rooted in the teachings of Vatican II that all genuine prayer is gift, covenant and communion with the triune God, D'Costa asks whether interreligious prayer is possible for loyal Christians. His conclusion is that such prayer, with certain boundaries, could be regarded as loving risk in the spirit of Jacob's wrestling with God in the night (Gen. 32.26).

In terms of 'gift', D'Costa emphasizes the humility that characterizes all prayer. The Church believes that the Holy Spirit, intrinsically related to Jesus, knows no bounds throughout cultures and religions. Pope John Paul II declared of the Assisi Day of Prayer that the Holy Spirit may actively inspire and move all genuine prayer. So D'Costa suggests Christians could benefit from learning prayer methods of Hindus and Buddhists, carefully incorporating them into Christian disciplines centred on the triune God. Although there are pitfalls, there are also advantages in that Christians may thereby bring to mind practices of prayer long forgotten in their own traditions. Further, he allows for the real possibility of recognizing the 'saints' of other faith traditions as examples of temples of the Holy Spirit, to whom Christians should show reverence and openness, 'cohabiting in the Spirit'. So, despite a number of warnings about judging the element of risk, D'Costa suggests there could be occasions – perhaps generated in times of crisis, need or suffering – when interreligious prayer 'might be the possible site for a mutual sharing of the gift of the Holy Spirit that might be present in the praying and prayers of others' (D'Costa, 2000, p. 153).

His second mark of true prayer is the covenant relationship that is the content of trinitarian ways of talking about God and the outcome of allowing oneself to be transformed by the Trinity. Loving relationship characterizes the practice of Jesus, through the Spirit's power, revealing the Father's love for Christians to be maintained as the 'Body of Christ'. D'Costa argues that because a covenant relationship exists between God and the whole creation, there is the possibility that this may also be true of God and all faiths. But if we suggest that all religions are praying to the same God, does that deny the uniqueness of faith in Christ and worship of the triune God? In highlighting the 'intentionality of the heart',

D'Costa recognizes a form of intentionality regarding the true 'object' of prayer that cannot be measured in terms solely of doctrinal correctness. Without denying the importance of conceptualizing knowledge, he allows for the uncontrollable movement of the Spirit in deliberately opening up a more holistic notion of proposition. Taking forward the overall argument of this chapter, D'Costa is avoiding the unhelpful polarizations of linking the possibility of interreligious prayer entirely with doctrinal assent or of a subjectivist-experiential communality.

D'Costa suggests a more interactive approach to dealing with propositional claims. If all genuine prayer is rooted in the Holy Spirit, its meaning cannot be regarded as fixed or static. Interreligious prayer, he argues, is both the gift (over which we have no control) of God's presence moving in our hearts to help us to a closer relationship with the triune God, and the offering of each participant. Muslims and Christians praying together – the psalms, the *Fatiha*, New Testament passages, or the Lord's Prayer – will have a different relationship with and set of meanings associated with the words: 'In this risky process, and in a way that cannot be predetermined, it may then be that both Muslim and Christian are praying, however *imperfectly* and *fragmentarily*, "with one accord"' (D'Costa, 2000, p. 160). So in terms of covenant relations, he argues for the possibility of a shared reverence for the same God, a common desire to follow God's will and so a sufficient co-intentionality to justify interreligious prayer.

In terms of the third mark of prayer – communion – D'Costa suggests the holding together of relations and the Trinity as a line of enquiry for grounds for interreligious prayer. Practically and doctrinally, real relations include both the overlap and difference that are signalled in speaking of the mutuality of trinitarian perichoretic relations. Finally he concludes that diving into the love of the triune God may include risking finding an even greater knowledge of the mystery and experience of the love of God through interreligious prayer:

> When interreligious prayer is done with a reverence and devotion to God in real love of God, with the consequent thirst for greater love between people, which always stems from and is nourished by a greater love of God, then in love's celebration of love by the lovers, we glimpse the reality of the Trinity in human community – even if not by common accord in name, but by one accord in the heart of love.
>
> (D'Costa, 2000, p. 165)

There are resonances here with Mary Grey's probing our understanding of God. She wonders whether the kenosis of God:

drives us towards our own self-emptying in order to encounter the beauty of other faiths, other cultural yearnings and manifestations of the sacred, and the empty middle deep in human longing. It can be no accident that the symbol of Divine vulnerability arises at a time when the violence of machoculture seems the main obstacle of re-encountering the intimacy of Jesus' relationship with the Father.

(Grey, 2000a, p. 31)

Conclusion

Sue Patterson reminds us that to be human is to be innovative:

To be born into and to continue life-long in the creative relation with words and things through which we participate in the making of both world and truth. This is the creaturely humanity which God has both made and embraced incarnationally; this, therefore, is the creaturely incarnation in which we participate in Christ.

(Patterson, 1999, p. 92)

I am deeply conscious that having opened a number of doors into highly specialist areas of literature and scientific endeavour, few today would claim the competence alone to interweave them at a deeper level. This has to be a corporate task. Others are and will be further exploring these and other avenues for re-imagining order, structure and relationality, which will encourage the mature articulation and practice of fundamentally new structures in church life. The search is for a new language in which the processes of church life can be reconceived as the vulnerable and coherent interplay of wholeness. My invitation is to local churches to know and celebrate the wide range of disciplines within which church members and sympathizers have vast expertise. Further my hope is that church leaders and congregations will – through one another – proactively draw out the dialogues that can enrich the Church's ability to recognize God at work and to move out to make rich and many-layered responses for the sake of the Kingdom. Experience reminds us that this process of making connections will require specific structures of meeting, learning and encouragement facilitated by church leaders: educators, bishops, ministry training directors, Readers and clergy.

No one form of insight or discipline should be seen as an exclusive way of helping us discover the best structures for understanding and living in the world. My own experience in training events for clergy and laity is that huge wells of untapped wisdom are present in the room. Recent education may have been focused in biblical studies, liturgy and doctrine, but many people have immense knowledge of music, artificial intelligence, physics, politics, education, child-rearing, ecology, management of people, finance, anthropology, drama, cooking and so on. I recall the thoughtful and excited rapport of a biologist responding to my attempts to open up the possibilities of trinitarian thought for concepts of relationships in Church and world. He was an expert in the year-in, year-out changes in Australian billabongs. Alternately wet and dried out, billabongs are to the casual observer apparently the same; yet in phenomenological observation they are renewed always differently. Daniel W. Hardy captures this spirit, as it relates to all creation including human persons:

> In the fabric of God's truth there is enough open texture left by the interweaving 'song of the Spirit' which is God's creative relation to the world for the arrangement of its factors not to be fixed, to allow us to develop creatively our own ways of living in the world.
>
> (Hardy, 1993, p. 71)

Each avenue of study – economics, ecology, social anthropology and so on – may act as a hologram for identifying ways of observing and making sense of reality.

David Bohm has made it clear that there can be no separation or fragmentation at the core of our thought and practice between the *content* and *function* of our ideas. So, to *talk* of a downward-stepped hierarchy in the Church will be inevitably to *live out* dependency; to practise worship in serried rows observing distant ritual will be unavoidably to convey a notion of a clerically displaced ministry. We have no choice but to live with our chosen ideas, so they had better be godly, beautiful and fruitful for all; our practice will be an open book for all to read, so it had better be mutually respectful and witnessing life in abundance for all. Field theories suggest that each interaction or location will be a hologram of the whole. We can make a start now to notice whether in our Church there are signs of God's Kingdom of radical inclusiveness and absence of permanent superordination when for worship, study, administration or relating to the world, there meet together children, women and men, rich and poor, those who are healthy and those with disabilities. The picture is probably one of volatile contradiction, which we shall disentangle only through sustained attention and dialogue. The resources we require lie in the thick, complex interweaving of particular kinds of knowledge that provide the wisdom for all living, which Christians understand as the relational energy of the triune God.

CHAPTER 3

Partnership in God's Mission

One of the deep background conclusions of my 'taking stock' in Chapter 1 was the potential for increasing confidence as a Church if we choose to let go of the status of marginalized victim and choose instead more boldly to discover diverse and holistic ways of re-imagining the Church. Faced with downward spirals of church allegiance and an ageing clergy, rather than looking for someone to blame and exclude, we could ask, 'What that is hopeful and fully alive, speaking of the liberating power of God, can our Church offer to people and a society searching for meaning in daily work and relationships?' I am aware of critically loyal church members who express frustration and abandonment in working for open communities that celebrate, examine, repair and continue to shape interactive patterns of communication between God, God's whole life in the world and all creation. An urgent question is: 'How does the Church that I need and of which I want to be a proud member and advocate, get to experience and serve "daily bread" that is fresh, nourishing and attractive?' And, more deeply and urgently, with Martin Luther King Jnr, 'Who is our God?' or 'Who is worshipped here?'

Many of the old Churches in Britain are experiencing the shame of being ignored in society now. We can easily feel overwhelmed when we contrast our Church with, say, a lively young pentecostalist congregation or the awareness that in Africa today huge crowds turn up for worship and open-air missions. Our context and opportunity is different, but we are still the Church of God, called not to fold our hands in helplessness but to rely on the miracle of God working though and among us. Walter Brueggemann, in his biblical studies, has reminded us that we worship the God of impossibilities, who 'does not quit even when the evidence warrants his quitting' (Brueggemann, 1978, p. 69).

Reflection on Jesus' preaching to and feeding the crowds despite trying to find some peace after the violent death of his cousin, John the Baptizer, reveals Christian ministry as giving even when we are not aware of having anything to give. In Matthew's account (14.13–20), the disciples experience themselves as empty-handed and sensing the utter impossibility of feeding the crowds. Jesus teaches them that even when the political situation is one that allows for the killing of John, a great prophet, the people need God's disciples to hear, see and feel with them. Some have suggested that Matthew's throwaway comment in counting the numbers fed – 'not counting women and children' – may reveal that as many as 35,000 were present in total – in a five or six to one ratio with 5,000 men. And so not only the disciples but also the children and women would be providers of food to share (see McKenna, 1994).

In the context of uncertainty and violent death that can flare up regularly in Kenya, and responding to Jesus feeding the crowds and teaching the disciples, Nyambura J. Njoroge urges:

> We must act! We have to show compassion, give what we have as well as lead the people to share whatever they have. It is a ministry with the people not a ministry *to* or for the people. There is no room for frozen disbelief and insensitivity like the one shown by the disciples when they suggested the crowds should be sent away. It is not just the material things we share but God's love and will for wholeness and wellbeing for all God's creation. Together we participate in feeding one another. This way the mission of God will be lived out by all the people of God in their everyday life.
>
> (Njoroge, 1998, p. 5)

I believe that although our inherited forms of Church in Britain and Europe are largely spent, we need not despair as though God no longer works wonders among us. We may be looking in the wrong places and not being prepared to co-operate with the dynamic of God's constant reordering. Biblical and theological discussion in the past 30 years have highlighted the inadequacy of so much of our inherited conceptions of Church and ministry, not least the dogmatic distinction between 'laity' and 'clergy'. Although the term 'laity' is derived from the Greek *laikos* – the most comprehensive term for all the members of God's people – it has taken on narrower connotations of those who are less significant and without competence. Scholars such as Ernst Käsemann, Hans Küng, G. W. H. Lampe and Ronald Fuller have for much of the past century revealed the problems entailed in thinking of Church primarily in terms of a clerical hierarchy and only subsequently as a faithful laity (Lampe, 1949).

So there exists within the Church a dualist split which is totally unbiblical, damages the Church's ability to be a reading of the Gospel to the world, and hinders the practice of mission. Our inherited words and experience of Church assume that ecclesiology has its logical starting place in what bishops and clergy say and do as God's representatives. My sense is that there remains a deep anxiety about taking as the ecclesiological starting point the truth that all Christians are laity (the royal priesthood, 1 Peter 2.5–9; Rev. 5.10) with gifts of the Spirit and a calling to take an equal part in the ministry of the 'handing over' of Christ's mission and ministry (Greek, *paradosis* of the *kerygma*). Not everyone is happy with the statement that ministry is the variegated form of the Church's entire existence as God's agent for the world's salvation (see Thurian, 1983, p. xvi).

In this chapter I want to explore the potential of a new theology and practice of Church capable of polymorphic variations as responses to God and God's life with us here and now. The Local Ministry movement – which in various parts of the world goes by the name of Total, Common, Mutual or Collaborative Ministry – offers, I believe, many clues of a grammar or way of perceiving a renewed paradigm of Church. We have seen in Chapter 2 that no theory really matches the reality of which we are speaking. But we have also seen that the ideas we espouse and the ways we live and work are intimately interwoven and co-create each other in one fluctuating process. Local Ministry emerges from, gives shape to and harnesses for action the energy of the great and varying pool of insight and experiment in the collaboration of ordained and non-ordained ministries for mission of recent decades. For me it carries the joyful possibility of working for and experiencing new ways of being Church that are more than fantasy. Small rural and inner-city parishes have found new vitality and confidence through revisiting what it means to say that baptism releases different and collaborative ministries in everyone.

The key to it is perhaps that Local Ministry takes us beyond the theologically impossible situation that God would leave us with a shortage of ministers. Apostolicity is transmitted through the entire Church. Christ is rooted in all the baptized; the ordained have a very particular contribution to the whole, but there is no authentic definition of deacon, priest or bishop that is not rooted in the work of all the baptized. Every Christian person, in their particular charism and integrated with everyone else, is set free to do what is necessary for the Church to be Church. This is not to deny the gift of ordination but to make it essential to re-explore what we mean by that and why, in the process of lifting the whole of creation to God, some Christian people are 'ordained'. Controversially but imaginatively, Zizioulas inevitably challenges the Church to find some other word for the particular contribution of deacon, priest and bishop, in linking baptism with the ordination of the entire eucharistic community for ministry: 'Through Ordination the Church becomes the community which relates the world to God – and this is essentially what mission should mean. Mission is not a method ... but an attribute related to the nature of the Church' (Zizioulas, 1985, pp. 224–5).

At Local Ministry conferences there is often laughter, flexibility, worship and spirituality that releases new energy, and an absence of gloom and blame. Here is both an emotional and thoughtful next step for Anglicans and all who value the combination of ordered spontaneity, equally rooted in the Church's earliest centuries and in human society now. In particular it carries the passionate and evangelical conviction of the ethic of ministry in the New Testament that is not bound to particular structures but is rather characterized in terms of brother- and sisterhood, service, opposition to isolation and rivalry and governed by the task of discipleship. It is also in the spirit of many loyal critics of the Church, such as Francis and his followers, John Wesley and his movement, and the base communities of Latin America and Africa, all of whom, naturally, espouse one or two paradigms of ministry that they sense have previously been neglected.

A critical reading of the history of ecclesiology sees it as a sequence of male creativity, revolt and revision (Watson, 2001). But the Local Ministry renovation of Church calls up the contributions of mystics and contemplatives among which number countless Christian women. Examples include: the confident assertion by Elisabeth Schüssler Fiorenza that 'Women *are* Church' equally included with men (Watson, 2001, p. 61); recent reworking of the Sophia tradition in the Judaeo-Christian literature by Elizabeth Johnson; the questioning of patriarchy by Letty Russell and Rosemary Radford Ruether; the re-appropriation of sexuality in the Church by Elisabeth Moltmann-Wendel and Carter Heyward; and the mystical tradition in the Middle Ages through Julian of Norwich and Hildegard of Bingen. They speak of a relational God shown to us in Jesus who calls all people out of fear and marginalization into transformative patterns of relating where just relationships are recognized as an embodiment of God's Kingdom: 'In the beginning was relation and in the relation is the power that creates the world, through us, and with us, and by us, you and I, you and we, and none of us alone' (C. Heyward, in Grey, 1997a, p. 37).

Local Ministry has the deep potential to be more than a scheme for keen parishes or the panacea to resolve all the Church's ills. Of necessity, in many forms it contains within it the seeds of a Church that instinctively picks up on the most truthful and liberating patterns of Christian living for both women and men, in diverse situations for our world now.

Is Local Ministry merely a practical strategy for survival? Well, yes, it can be and, as observation shows, it has been hijacked as a conservative way of clinging on to inherited patterns of parish ministry for a while longer. 'Are you short of clergy and money? Then reach for ways of "using" loyal laity to "help" the ailing or overworked clergy.' Certainly its present focus is usually on the development of the ministry for mission of all who choose to share in local worshipping communities.

This is not to deny the value of chaplaincies of many kinds or of those contacts the Church has with society best offered at diocesan or regional level. And yes, at its richest it refuses the tidy uniformity and incipient patriarchy and clericalism of inherited ministerial patterns. But what one will call 'mission strategy' another will call 'panic response to financial and numeric recession'. Local Ministry is certainly *both* of these and many other things besides. So when has there been a Church that wasn't riddled with paradoxes and mixed motives? Those who have experienced the fruits of this movement first-hand, however, usually demonstrate signs of a deepening spirituality and light-headedness that is interactive rather than a polarizing of apparent opposites. The Local Ministry movement buys a revolutionary freedom to explore many connections between faith and life, emphasizing how to have a sense of well-being, celebration, hope and enjoyment.

But is it an inward-looking strategy? We are right to have the recurring anxiety that when the Church attends energetically to the renewal of its life in the locality, everything else can be sacrificed, especially the call for laity to witness in the everyday. In the past 50 years, the Church of England has produced a forest of strategies and reports – such as *Toward the Conversion of England, All are Called: Investors in People in the Church*, and *Called to New Life: The Parish and People Movement* – to support people in living out the gospel in the whole of life. Levels of resistance are astonishingly vertiginous. Despite Ernie Southcott's passionate plea for the altar on Sunday to be the workbench on Monday, the Parish and People Movement will be remembered more for its liturgical innovations and its massaging of church-centred ministries (Southcott, 1966).

I know that as a diocesan missioner my efforts to persuade people to 'make connections' between worship, the triune God and everyday responsibilities produced fewer results than my interventions to promote personal spiritual growth or the development of parish life. Maybe I misread the best place for intervention. There are no guarantees. History may yet label 'Local Ministry' as simply the last jar on the shelf in the twentieth-century Church's corner shop of remedies for religious ennui.

To try to avoid such a disastrous waste of imagination and energy I believe we need the ventilation that results from deliberately sharing in the international ecumenical discourse on 'Why Church?' I want to sidestep adversarial competition between parish and chaplaincy, between one set of fashionable strategic language and another, and certainly any utopian notion of linear developmental success – 'Just one more push on the Local Ministry bandwagon and the Kingdom of God will appear'. The bottom line is what kind of Church – in manifold forms and social contexts – is required if we are more confidently to participate in the mission of God in the world?

In the previous chapter we explored briefly how a growing number of scientists and theorists are dreaming of and working for a future for the world that assumes that everything affects everything else. In Chapter 4 I shall be examining in detail strategies from several dioceses of the Anglican Communion for signs of trustworthy ways of re-imagining Church that resonate with a holistic understanding of reality. In the remainder of this chapter I want to suggest how to sketch out some of the current international and ecumenical priorities for developing theories of mission in the local church. I believe they reflect the overall approach of Chapter 2 in that in themselves they imply a spirit of interconnectedness, and that separately and together they offer imaginative lines of enquiry for a future Church.

I write with two clear underlying presuppositions. First, that local churches – alone or in clusters, ecumenically where possible – have the capability of becoming the search engine for Christians to make many fruitful connections between worship and the development of their response to God's call to share in working for the coming of the Kingdom, in whatever places of influence they occupy. There need be no false dichotomies between the practice of church community and society. The true prophets I have known became incandescent *precisely* because they were rooted in a disciplined, open, worshipping community. At their best, Christian spirituality and Church praxis allow for the proper ebb and flow of inner and outer community living. There is no either/or between the hospitality of the liturgy and the search for justice and peace, between prayer and work or personal and corporate:

> The spirit of hope works through every reality, religious, spiritual, cultural, socio-economic and political in their cosmic dimensions. Hope through Spirit permeates the whole creation for the inner reality of human beings to the outer reality of this whole creation (Gal. 5.5; Rom. 15.13; 8.19–21).
>
> (Yong-Bock, in Fergusson and Sarot, 2000, p. 119)

Second, and closely related, the Church lives out its calling equally and differently in a polyphony of locations: in school, prison, industrial chaplaincy, university and college, cathedral, friendship and family, neighbourhood, community or among those with a disability, cell group and local church; through ecological concern, scientific disciplines, literature, music, arts, psychology, therapies and healing, pastoral care, communication and celebrations.

So Jean Vanier speaks of countercultural L'Arche communities, which embrace weakness, live out non-manipulative lives, see, appreciate and develop gifts in others and ourselves, and respect difference, admit errors and live in risk-taking intimacy (Vanier, 1999, pp. 57–61). Each needs all the others to know its true self. None can say, 'Because you are not me, you are not required.'

Theories and practice of local churches of mission will need to flow out of exploration in the overlapping areas I will now delineate.

A Church in which everyone counts

Whatever its virtues, the inherited imbalanced and restricted patterns of Church, centred in a solo aristocratic or expert priestly ministry, is not enough – given all the other information we now have. There are three reasons for this. It is rooted in the extremely limited linear understanding of God's life with the world. Second, it works effectively in only the simplest social situations and in the complex social life of today invites ordained ministry to do the impossible or to reduce the range of tasks to be undertaken to those that a traditional priesthood can manage or direct. Lastly, implying that the priest directly represents Christ in the community, it subverts the sharing in the messianic identity of Jesus Christ of all the baptized, requiring laity to be subjects of an impoverished vision of Church necessitated by the limited vision of overworked clergy. So the consequences for God, God's mission and the ministry of the Church are extremely serious.

Invited to look ahead to the future of the Church in questions after giving a lecture in London in September 2000, Jürgen Moltmann placed emphasis on the sense of being needed. From his personal observation of church life in Germany, he emphasized the importance of church communities that expect everyone to make a contribution: 'It matters that you are here.' He suggested that anonymous churches that don't really mind whether you're there or not, except to boost numbers and finances, and that basically rely on the ordained minister and a band of loyal helpers are not likely to be around for very much longer. The Local Ministry spirit dances with those in every generation who have looked for a Christian community where everyone recognizes their personal and corporate invitation – as one of the Desert Fathers suggested – to be turned into a pillar of fire.

The context for new thinking

Rapid change is one of the most frequent topics of writing, discussion and anguish in the world and Church today: chaos theory, 'post-modernism', contemporary films, literature, philosophy, quantum theory, field theory and engagement with the idea of a new millennium all suggest in different ways that the mechanical certainties of modernity are coming unstuck (see Borgmann, 1992; Lakeland, 1997; and Tanner, 1997). The Western cultural polarizations that used to be taken for granted – between mind and body, worship and social responsibility, adult and child, reason and emotion, academic and experiential, content and process, theory and practice, tradition and spontaneity, male and female, clergy and lay, real and fictional, science and religion, sacred and secular, praise and lament, fact and value, truth and myth, inner and outer, absolute and relative – are no longer subtle enough to help us interpret the realities that constitute daily experience.

As we saw in Chapter 2, although quantum theorists have a long way to advance before they receive a general acceptance, their belief that the whole is greater than the sum of the parts resonates with a Church of creativity, uncertainty, warmth, process, intimacy, learning, nearness, the possibility of participation, and a responsibility for being part of all creation. In modern physics the image of the universe as a machine composed of separate pieces has been transcended by the alternative perception of an indivisible dynamic whole whose parts are essentially interrelated and can be understood only as patterns of a cosmic process. As Fritz Capra has put it, 'There is motion, but ultimately no moving objects; there are no dancers; there is only the dance itself!' There are no mere observers. 'Participator' is the incontrovertible new concept given by quantum mechanics. It strikes down the term 'observer' of classical theory, the one who stands safely behind the thick glass wall and watches what goes on without taking part. That just can't be done.

Scientists and therapists who in recent years have given us the principles of field theory draw our attention to how reality can be explored and known only when it is recognized as a field of interaction, never static or predictable and always responding to new circumstances. Learning organization theorists commend a way of institutional life where people continually expand their capacity to create the results they truly desire, where new and expansive patterns of thinking are nurtured. A learning company concerned with whole systems development is defined by one of the leading groups of writers as one that 'facilitates the learning of all its members and consciously transforms itself and its context' (Pedler, Burgoyne and Boydell, 1997, p. 3).

Many laity in the Church will be working every day in the modelling processes of the learning organization. It would be naive to assume the Church would flourish by simply adopting its principles. The more realistic likelihood is that the opportunity for engagement with them will hardly be faced. Some of the characteristics commonly associated with the learning company have slogans that I believe have intriguing links with the language for exploring a future Church. For example, a learning company questionnaire uses 11 headings, which are listed here, slightly amended: a learning approach to strategy; participative policy-making; informing everyone; accounting and control linked with the overall vision; internal exchange rather than top-down control; reward for flexibility; structures that enable; those on the boundary recognized as holding valuable information to be fed into policymaking; inter-company learning; a climate of continuous creativity; and self-development opportunities for everyone. I want to emphasize that this is only one avenue of exploration and it would be crass to imagine that here lies all necessary wisdom. My concern is rather that we might be more likely to say that here lies no wisdom for Churches, whatsoever.

Changes facing the Church itself

Do the main British Churches really have a future while hanging on to the notion and practice that their chief ministers are the ordained? We have noted in Chapter 1 how Churches are facing immense challenges – diminishing membership; growing marginalization; buildings experienced more as a problem than a resource; fewer people offering themselves as parish priests; numbers of clergy due for retirement in the next five to ten years out of all proportion with the numbers currently being ordained; many ordinands already at life's meridian, so offering fewer years of service; income from all sources no longer enough to pay the bills; and in some dioceses clergy housing falling below acceptable standards of repair.

In summary, it's as though we're pretending, against all the evidence, that there are still enough clergy and resources to maintain the inherited pattern of Church – rather than hearing God's invitation and using our imaginations to reinvent ourselves in untraditional ways. By inherited patterns I mean the kind of Church that's like a pub or a post office in that if you want certain services you turn up and buy what you want without commitment. It would be laughable to imagine the national brewery needs my love or involvement. The fantasy seems to be that we can go on pretending that we still have just enough people and money to survive without radical change or without taking an urgent but profound look at the question, 'Why Church at all?'

Theological grounding

A deeper understanding of how Churches can serve God's mission begins from exploring four interrelated themes.

Echoing the Trinity

A Church that recognizes that its present forms are dying needs to throw itself on God. The psalmists remind us to trust God's saving power now and to make daring appeals to God, simply because God is known to be merciful and gracious and has worked wonders in the past. 'For you are great and do wondrous things; you alone are God' (Ps. 86.10). Jürgen Moltmann has reminded us of the inexhaustible mystery of God who is inexpressibly beyond us as well as closer to us than our own breath. Moltmann shows how before the resurrection Jesus lives from works of the creative Spirit; after the resurrection the order becomes Father, Son, Spirit, for Jesus becomes a source of energy and joins in the sending of the Spirit to varying communities of disciples; in transforming and bringing the whole of creation and bringing it into God's final future the order in God is Spirit, Son, Father, for the Spirit is the energy of the new creation and brings all to new life (Moltmann, 1989a). The different pattern of relation within God and God's self-communication – in the Christian tradition we call 'Trinity', three persons relating in dynamic community – is at present rekindling the imagination of many who are struggling to hear the Church's future for the world's sake.

The Brazilian Franciscan theologian Leonardo Boff notably invites Christians to enquire reverently into God's character and way of working in creation, to understand our lives as those who are visited by and drawn into the life of the trinitarian communion of God, and to explore what type of society – in our context – accords with God and God's plan (Boff, 1992). The doctrine of the Trinity revolutionizes how we think of God and what it means to be human. It has the capacity to critique and renovate all forms of life together in the light of the God revealed in Jesus through the Spirit. Now is the time to discover a revitalized way of thinking about God that can take us on from those linear ways of structuring Church and life that were not derived from our knowledge of God's life as an overflowing communion of difference in relation:

> A unitarian, patriarchal, monarchical, hierarchical theism gradually replaced a trinitarian mono-theism, with disastrous, political results. Christian theologians justified every kind of hierarchy, exclusion and pattern of domination, whether religious, sexual, clerical, racial as 'natural' and divinely intended.
>
> (LaCugna, 1992, p. 17)

Recent ecumenical work on the structure, ecumenical ministry and authority of the Church have drawn on a renewed trinitarian theology to explore new models of collaboration as characteristic of the Church (see, for example, British Council of Churches, 1991; House of Bishops, 1997; and Bishops' Conference of England and Wales, 1995). I believe it is already playing a part in moving dioceses, in their prayer and worship and first tentative stages of new thought, away from hierarchical models of Church. It invites us to a more relational understanding and therefore encourages a mutual approach to ministry. So the Diocese of Birmingham writes:

> In faith we understand the life of God the Holy Trinity to be a life in perfect relationship. The gracious mystery of the life of God is the very bedrock of our life and witness as the Church. In this our hope for the future lies. Mutuality, collaboration, co-working are basic themes of this report for they are ways in which we seek to give expression to what God-in-Trinity asks of us in this time of decision.
>
> (*Shaping Ministry*, 1999)

In recent decades, mainstream Christian theology has declared its restored belief in the Trinity as the heart of expressing belief in God (see Gunton, 1998). This faith – hard won from reflection on Scripture, through prayer, worship, everyday living and the experience of belonging to Christian communities – invites continued further exploration (Ford and Stamps, 1996). Rather than seeing trinitarian relatedness as a dusty and irrelevant excavation from the early Church, and a safe if static bulwark of orthodoxy, we could try entering into it now as though standing on the edge of the future. Now is an opportune time to make connections between our understanding of God and the character of the Church (see LaCugna, 1992, pp. 376ff.). To know the quality and complexity of relatedness to which the Spirit invites us in church communities will require some deep diving into the life of God.

The Greek word *perichoresis* has been used to talk of the relatedness of God as three coequal persons in the freedom of genuine community (see John 17.20–1). So Boff can explicitly hope for Churches with structures that model immediacy, face-to-face presence and reciprocity as advance signs of a human society free of injustice and oppression. 'Communion requires being-in-openness (freedom), being-in-transcendence (ecstasis), and being us (the new ontological reality created by persons in communion)' (Boff, 1992, pp. 130f.).

Boff regards the trinitarian God as the infinite exemplification of absolute openness, supreme presence, total immediacy, eternal transcendence and infinite communion. This is what God is – communion of difference. We should not get caught up in the 'threeness' of a trinitarian paradigm. Rather it points to the dynamic quality, the interrelation of a number of persons, places and roles that together constitute a rich wholeness. These insights lead to the demand for dialogue with many disciplines – precisely because we work with the canvas of the whole of God's life in the whole of God's world.

Incarnated – working with God's life in the world

The question must be faced time and time again, 'What is the form of Christ in the world?' (Anderson, 1999). Christian theology and practice is always earthed in the particulars of time and place. The Anglican preoccupation with engaging with God in the particulars of each locality can still serve into the foreseeable future if we persist in imaginatively reinventing the parish tradition in untraditional ways (Holloway, 1999). In the mobile society of today most people will draw their identity from belonging to a cluster of localities. For example, there are those who will be worshipping on a Sunday, working through the week and living in their home, all three of which are in separate locations with potentially conflicting allegiances. This complex situation often leads to a compartmentalization forcing a separation between where one lives, works and worships. Further, every locality – of worship, work and home – is in fact increasingly experienced as diverse and possibly in adversarial conflict, a consequence of which will often be a refusal to make connections between these core places.

Part of the subversive character of the Church is to continue reshaping itself in order to show society its true life, through making creative connections between the worlds of work, home and faith. This calls for the reconstruction of ecclesiology in such a way that it can draw into dynamic interaction worship, spirituality, the building up of a faith community and an engagement with the world with the expectation of calling out one another in love to be what God intends. In this incarnational approach the model for all ministry is the self-emptying of Christ. Sharing in Christ, those who wash one another's feet as a command of the Lord are so to be drawn into God's trinitarian life that we are formed equally by Christ and by the Spirit, by the memory of the life of Jesus and his dynamic presence now, by the life of worship and the prophetic life as sign of the final end of creation.

Mary Grey has reflected on the present inability of the Church's worship to inspire the body, mind and heart of the majority of people, and the Church's inability to initiate the young 'into a sense of awe, wonder, connectedness and responsibility for the sacredness of existence' (Grey, 2000b, p. 44). Yet, as Brueggemann (1978) reminds us, we are inheritors of a great tradition that interweaves the pursuit of holiness with midwifing justice and peace. The potential of the Local Ministry movement is to make prophetic connections between liturgy as genuine 'people's work' and the work of the Church as sacrament or sign of God's coming Kingdom in every field of human endeavour. This requires the deliberate shaping of a Church after the likeness of the Trinity; as an authoritative manifestation of God's hope; as a distinctive, Spirit-led, company of subversives. In this we are needing to create for ourselves the foundations of a way of being Church (ecclesiology) that links the dangerous memory of Jesus Christ with a wild dreaming of what communities may become. This is also to transcend tired debates as to whether Church is about being or doing. In a trinitarian understanding, the Church moves beyond such polarizations to a more dynamic flow as both word and sign, proclamation and icon of Christ's life in the world.

And for this we shall have to subvert the expertise of clergy and accredited ministers, except as those who place themselves humbly in the context of the powerlessness experienced by others and in that situation share their particular insights and prophetically encourage others to do the same. Instead of incoming clergy consciously or unconsciously requiring the amateur status to meet their own expertise, we need to foster an ecology where each knows truly their own place and respects their uniquely different knowledge. The late Brazilian educationalist, Paulo Freire, author of *Pedagogy of the Oppressed*, recounts in a later work how, faced with the silence of his audience in the face of his overwhelming power, he sets up a game in which he will be the loser. He seeks to empower the poor by deliberately setting himself up to reveal his limited knowledge in a question-and-answer game in which they asked him only about what they knew from their local experience (see Grey, 1999, pp. 335ff.).

A local church is unavoidably part of its own context. As a privileged agent of God's hope it will also need to be growing in awareness itself within its context so that there can be a genuine ministry to the whole of the place and the community of communities of which the Church is a part. What are people going through here at the present time? What are they suffering? What do they have to celebrate? What are the important relationships? What do differing groups understand as local? How can a local church serve a neighbourhood where differing social groups espouse competing notions? There will be several distinct notions of ministry at work in a village, quite unconsciously adopted by different groups of residents. Some believe the church is there for them, but it's not their place to presume to run it – that's the vicar's job; others want a church that fulfils their nostalgia with a vicar, bells and matins, and yet others look for a 'committed' church in which those who have come to faith celebrate a risen Lord and proclaim him to those of their neighbours who will respond (Jenkins, 1999). The language and social activities each group will see as appropriate and the persons they would accept as proper to perform church activities will also vary hugely. So any talk of 'local ministry' will inevitably give off a spectrum of signals even in one locality. In field theory, all are necessary for each other (see Hiley and Peat, 1998; and Marshall and Zohar, 1997).

The challenge might be to ask whether they are prepared to recognize and listen to each other rather than merely to demonize the other groups. Churches at their best aspire to being multilingual and prepared to engage with society on other people's terms – music, ecology, social justice, education or information technology. Each of us is called uniquely to share responsibility for mission of this quality (see O'Murchu, 1997).

As disciples of the historical, suffering Jesus as well as of the risen Christ, we are summoned to discover a practical-prophetic ecclesiology for which each will have a difficult and particular responsibility. Following Christ in gratitude we are called to play a unique part in the drama made possible by Christ, in free interaction with all other disciples. A key ingredient of the Church's task we find is 'to help discover what our particular role is and to help us to play it better' (Healy, 2000, p. 65).

Sharing God's mission

A third keynote is the call of the whole Church to mission – participating in God's mission in the world. Dioceses and local churches do seem more focused now on reviewing their ordinary living in terms of the mission of God's love to the world; they are working out practical, holistic tactics in line with their key principles.

The Church is but a means to an end, not an end in itself. The end is that God's Kingdom may come on earth as it is in heaven (Diocese of Derby). Our aim is to develop vibrant, inclusive, attractive Christian communities. That succinctly expresses the view of Lesslie Newbigin that the only effective interpreter of the gospel today is a congregation of men and women who believe it and live by it (Diocese of Peterborough). God, the Creator of all, both permits the creation freely to develop, and at the same time has a passionate loving intention towards it. This final purpose is made known to human beings through God's revelation and is offered to us to share in. The purpose of God, as expressed in Ephesians, is a new creation where all things are brought together and there is complete harmony between created order and Creator. The Church of God then, does not have a mission, but the God of mission has a church. Mission stems from what we understand to be the dynamic interplay of the persons of the Trinity. In the documents of the Diocese of Wakefield we find the idea that the creative work of the Holy Trinity in the people of God should be foremost and permanent. The institutions that are the scaffolding for this life should be secondary and changing.

The coming of the year 2000 has taken up a great deal of energy that may obscure the true Christian interest in the last things. In planning how to be Church, eschatology constitutes a primary key. We can understand the passing away of the old world and the coming of the new like the resurrection of the crucified and dead Christ, as a process of divine transformation and transfiguration. Paul in Romans 8 imagines the pains of the decline of this world as something like the birth pangs of God's new world. In the biblical traditions, world history does not begin with the Fall and therefore does not end with the destruction of the world either. It begins with the original blessing of the temporal creation and ends with the bliss of the eternal creation. 'See, I am making all things new' (Rev. 21.5). That is the 'new heaven and the new earth' which are to come when 'the first heaven and the first earth' pass away (Rev. 21.1). We can interpret the local Christian community as an agent of change, becoming, however partially, a sign and foretaste of God's passionate desire for the fulfilment of all creation in justice, reconciliation, and kaleidoscopic harmony.

A key question to any local church, therefore, is: 'How do you see yourselves as participating in God's future now?' It might be about local community involvement about racism or inadequate housing and family life; or it might be about world debt and international justice and it will mean including the poor, the sick and the ones pushed to the edge of society – rather than just patronizing them from a distance. Vergilio Elizondo writes with passion:

> The poor may not be excluded from this task [of being Church]. Since they see better than others the prison from which humanity is to be freed, and hence have a better grasp of God's redemptive will and power, they are in a privileged position for hearing God's word. 'God has chosen what is foolish in the world to shame the wise, God has chosen the weak in the world to shame the strong, God has chosen what is low and despised in the world ... to bring to nothing things that are' (1 Cor.1. 27–28).
>
> (Elizondo, 1999, p. 109)

How is a Church sharing Christ's love in action by engaging with God's active presence in the particular and ordinary? How can this Church be an embodiment of the Lord's prayer – your Kingdom come on earth – here?

Or, taking Matthew's challenge, where are you for the poor, the naked, the prisoner and the sick?

Even if haltingly, we still sense what is our task – to be responsible together for living God's life and work among us and showing it in the world; through our worship, ministry and common life to be one and holy and to extend this into the world. But we must go much further. 'If we are the circle of God's life in the world, how do we restore that circle and make it a deepening spiral of participation in the life of God in the world? Is it not too much to ask that we get our act together, and do the job properly!' (Hardy, 1996, pp. 221f.).

Baptism – keystone of the Christian experience of communion

A fourth frequent theological theme (again reflecting much recent ecumenical theology) is that *baptism* is the basis for being part of the Church. Baptism – for those who choose to accept it – provides the basic qualification for ministry and confers on all those who are baptized the responsibility for developing their own ministry within the whole mission of the people of God. The ministry of all the baptized is exercised by the Church not only when gathered together but also when dispersed in the life of the world. All share in the task of theological reflection. All must share in scrutinizing the signs of the times in the light of context, Scripture tradition and worship, to discover God's will now.

On the basis of common baptism, all have become priests, and all realize this priesthood in their own way on the basis of their respective charismata. Hence all members of the Church, both office holders and 'laypersons', are fundamentally equal (Volf, 1998, p. 246). Across the world, ecumenically, books, journals, conferences and official texts explore how the ministry and mission of the Church belongs to the whole Christian community and not just to the few who are ordained. The Second Vatican Council (1962–6) rediscovered *koinonia* (communion, fellowship, mutual participation) as a primary building block for understanding what it is to be Church – communion, community, communication (*Lumen Gentium*, 1995). In the World Council of Churches Lima Texts – *Baptism, Eucharist and Ministry* (1982) – and the 1991 Canberra Assembly Declaration, and more recently the Porvoo and other Reports of ecumenical dialogue, *koinonia* is developed as a basic ecclesiological category. Unity through difference replaces consensus, which eliminates diversity. Lambeth Conferences as far back as 1920 emphasized baptism as the foundation of an Anglican understanding of ecclesiology (see House of Bishops, 2001, para. 12).

Four interlocking themes of baptism draw out its significance for this discussion. Baptism: brings the one being baptized into intimate connection with the death and resurrection of Jesus Christ; grants incorporation in the triune life of God and the Christian community; is a commissioning, in company with all other baptized people, for working for the fulfilment of God's mission; and is inaugurated eschatology. Through accepting both resurrection faith and the challenge to wrestle with all that brings down people and creation, we are agents and signs already of what God will have in the end.

The challenge is that as a baptized Christian, I am already commissioned as part of Christ's own ministry. Whether I am ordained or not is immaterial. No matter how I react, the statement remains true. I may be surprised, alarmed, pleased, antagonized, suspicious, acquiescent, scornful or enraged. Nevertheless, by baptism I share in the ministry of Christ. This demands the developing of Churches in which we find new language that goes beyond the 'clerical'–'lay' divide. And to reach that point all Christian people will need to be better nurtured in taking hold of their ministerial responsibility both for doing their Christian living in the networks of the everyday and to take part in redeveloping the Church in mission. And only when their Church requires of them that they see their sharing of the life of the streets and shops, of wrestling with issues of land, feeding, housing, business, and unemployment, and issues about race, justice, drug abuse, sexuality and so on as their Christian ministry will they begin to be effective. For then through the Holy Spirit they will consciously bring blessing, forgiveness and the sacrifice of Christ for the world. Our task now is to let go of old securities and work for an identity that will, like Jesus, comfort and heal the needs and conflicts around us. Or else our hope will appear impotent and as a Church we shall deserve to die (see J. B. Metz, 1980, pp. 136ff.).

Bishops, priests and deacons will have to be reinvented – indeed to judge from the vast current literature the process is at an advanced stage. Early church studies fundamentally agree that among the first Christians, in contrast to Judaism, there was an avoidance of designating those who performed functions to enable the Church to happen by titles that set them apart or gave superior rank (Barnett, 1995, ch. 1). Naturally in the course of time sophisticated organizational patterns have emerged but there is no reason to abandon the principle of a fundamental equality among the Christian assembly. What we currently call 'ordained' ministry has to be reconceived in ecclesiological and corporate terms. It is one of the fundamental supports and constitutive foci for the development of the Church's identity as a multitude of callings and gifts. The picture of Jesus making special demands on the twelve as both representatives and members of the renewed Israel is an important insight into the particular ministry of bishop, priest and deacon. The Lima Texts speak of all the ordained as assisting the whole Church through being heralds, leaders and pastors.

There is certainly in the New Testament a significant thread of commissioning, being asked to act on behalf of God, Christ or the Church, which is a key element in 'ordained' ministry set within the Church for its flourishing (see, for example, Matt. 10.1–8; Luke 10.16; 24.47; John 20.21; 2 Cor. 5.20). However, all authority has to be received and is therefore dialogical and persuasive in character. In an ecclesiology rooted in baptism rather than a hierarchy of the ordained, there is a special and distinctive place for the ordained but never as to subvert the apostolic task of all. So clergy are not called on to perceive themselves alone as experts in the inherited sense, on worship, Scripture, spiritual guidance and preaching. Experts today will understand how groups work, the various methods of adult education, and how to serve that expertise interactively, not imposing or dominating. No one is called just to sit and listen; everyone in their own way is called to think, dream, imagine, explore, decide and act. No one is discounted because of their age, educational experience, social status or gender. Christian adult education must not be limited to evening classes for the leisured individual and elite enquirer.

Edward Schillebeeckx, a leader of ministry development thought in the 1970s and 1980s, expressed sadness that in Holland a great opportunity for diversifying education had been missed by 'making all ministers academics' (Schillebeeckx, 1980, p. 84). Gustavo Gutiérrez and Elisabeth Schüssler Fiorenza seek to identify future forms of *ekklesia* as faith communities of decision-making individuals identifying with the oppressed and seeking justice. They have spoken out for all those who knowingly or not have experienced the tyranny and silencing of forms of theological education that were just not appropriate for them. They ask whose wisdom is excluded or included by the dominant paradigm of knowledge (see Grey, 1999, pp. 338ff.). We must learn from this. We need a vision for learning processes for local Christian communities that point to a future beyond complex systems of dominance, however benign, as the tool by which God's Kingdom can be established on earth (Bacon and Jobling, 2001, p. 102). Those who can assist others to do 'process' will take trouble to know the immediate needs of people locally including the struggle of the non-person for justice, liberation, salvation and well-being; they will offer short courses of immediate and obvious value; they will make no one feel foolish or inadequate; they are flexible to stretch everyone into becoming an expert; and they will transform, liberate and energize groups of people together to see wider horizons and ways of serving God's purposes.

The transformative educational energy that local churches require to become communities of face-to-face intimacy with God, one another and society has hardly yet begun to be explored. Some with responsibility for developing theological education for mission and ministry that leads to transformative action are engaging with the work of Paulo Freire and with what James Loder calls 'four-dimensional knowing, involving the lived world, the self, the void and the holy', and Craig Dystra terms 'imaginal transformation' (Johns, 1999). In *The Ministry Team Handbook* (2000), I outlined two possible ways for a Christian community to deepen its sense of vocation and explore how it is sharing in God's life in the world. The first is a model that looks simultaneously in four directions: to the Judaeo-Christian inheritance and the diverse experiences of the earliest Christians; to the work of the Spirit in worship, transformation and community now; to the present context with all its human insights; and to the Church's vocation within God's final purposes for all creation. The second, acknowledging the work of Stanley Hauerwas (Ford and Stamps, 1996), suggests that the many points within the shape of the Eucharist provide natural springboards into liberation theology and action.

Theories of mission and pleas for evangelism require the partnership of some human honesty. Who are we choosing to exclude – as church gatekeepers? Do we truly want to make space for people? This means working for openness to many different approaches to planning celebrations of the Eucharist, to the use of buildings, to exploring faith and everyday life, to relating the energy of a local church to its physical and human context, to recognizing and empowering gifts of ministry. I always remember the amazement in a man who had previously only known very buttoned-up formal worship, when he stood around a kitchen table experiencing the power of the sharing of God's Word and the bread and wine in that context. That may not sound very profound, but I believe we deserve a Church that can speak aptly to the many and various parts of ourselves and of our society on different occasions, within the unity of God's life in the world (see Morisy, 1997).

Summary

The task of the local church – in all its manifestations – is to practise community: first, as a doctor practises medicine, the Church practises community, following the example and in communion with Jesus Christ; second, the sinful and divided Church has only the capacity to practise – it is far from achieving perfection; third, this practice is not to create an insular community but rather to demonstrate and evoke – however partially – the practice of community in all the networks of society.

I believe current debates about mission highlight the tension between the Church doing what it does for reasons entirely internal to its own nature and history and the attempt to listen and respond to the presence and working of God in every dimension of the life of society. Much has been written lately from the parish perspective – in all its diversity. Where are the voices reflecting on these same international and ecumenical theological issues in the contexts of hospitals, industry, schools, prisons and shopping centres? What kind of local church are they? What identity, with what kind of relationships, internally and externally, would a Church need to assume to be likely to embody the spiritual quest of more people in our society today? What kind of learning for everyone will be needed and where will be most appropriately resourced?

The Church that mostly now fails to refresh the inner parts mercifully has no future. Something new is called for if we're up for it. Abandoning defensiveness, considering what are acceptable insights and hopes among people generally, using every imaginative muscle, and in conversation with God, multidimensional Christian Churches can contribute to the quest for the fullest and more truthful developments of creation – what Christ called being a citizen of God's Kingdom.

CHAPTER 4

Five Diocesan Ministry Strategies

Introduction

The term 'strategy' may seem to some too harsh or pedestrian a word for the discussion of our receiving of God's grace and our participation in the mission of God in the world. Yet in my experience as a ministry officer, the lack of an agreed, however temporary and versatile, plan (and in particular the absence of a widely debated and corporately recognized statement on ministries to serve a vision for mission locally), can cause immense frustration and severely reduces the energy available. In this chapter I want to report and comment briefly on the attempts by five dioceses in very different parts of the Anglican Communion to produce strategic plans. In the quest for a post-hierarchical Church I believe we have a particular need to observe how essential is the commitment of bishops and arch-deacons and educational and ministerial developers together to support new steps. Where this partnership and commitment is absent, the work of developing partnership in ministry locally is very hard indeed.

I suggest that the process of distilling and then achieving a consensus for such plans permits the development of clear criteria for answering questions about the nature and vital role of the bishops and archdeacons in the present reformation of Anglicanism. This process also provides criteria against which to ask pointed questions about clergy numbers, the identity, selection and training of clergy, budgeting, the nature of authority and authorization in collaborative teams, the role of Readers and the task of the local church itself. I also have in mind the widely held belief today that, since the tasks to be performed in church life are always changing with differing situations, there is no fixed number of gifts or ministerial patterns. New ones emerge in response to new needs. Paul's list in 1 Corinthians 12 lays no claim to be definitive for all time. Not all the gifts he mentions there will be necessary for every period in the Church's life. One of Paul's key points is that all ministries exist in communion with the others and therefore the proper starting point is not with the individual but with the needs and calling of the whole body or community (see Moltmann, 1977, pp, 300ff.).

The examples given below also highlight the importance of inventing new models of collaboration and continuity in diocesan structures to give encouragement to laity and clergy attempting to find workable and sustainable structures locally.

Diocese of Pretoria, Southern Africa

Addressing an in-service clergy conference in the Diocese of Moray, Ross and Caithness in 1999, the then Suffragan Bishop of Pretoria, Robin Briggs, painted a picture of their search for a new way of being Church. This report of the ministry for mission strategy in Pretoria derives from his personal and lively account, part story and part concept. Fully supported by the diocesan bishop Richard Kraft, Robin identified his way of being bishop 'as a travelling pastor – an encourager, uniter (representing the larger Church to each small unit) and vision-sharer, challenger, among often struggling communities and thin on the ground compared with other denominations'.

In the diocese as a whole, there numbered 146 clergy in parish ministry (22 stipendiary and 124 self-supporting), together with many trained voluntary lay workers and two bishops in active ministries of support. In that year the diocesan budget was set at £300,000. Sociologists, economists and theologians had presented the tough reality that much of Southern Africa would be likely to become poorer while a small minority would continue to enjoy most of the wealth. So the burning question was, 'Which reality do we prepare the Church for?' The answer has to be a poorer Southern Africa, especially the vast – often invisible to the city dwellers – economically deprived rural and marginal areas. The bishop described how professional clergy have expectations of surviving 'with dignity with computers, health clubs, a decent house and kitchen, indoor heating, a modern car, medical facilities and good education for their children'.

Whereas 25 years ago it took the tithes of, say, 70 families – an average strong parish congregation – to support each stipendiary priest, leaving something over for the diocese and its staff, in the present economic situation it takes between 120 and 150 tithing units – found in only 10 per cent of parishes now – to keep the Church that is dependent on stipendiary priests. So, Pretoria has no choice but to be radical, and seek to build instead an indigenous Church.

Witbank is a vacant parish, growing fast, cared for by a self-supporting priest (a printer), a retired lay minister who is preparing for ordination, and an eager team. Nearby Middelburg, also a mining town, has a rector and deacon, both retired early, basically self-supporting, trained by the diocesan Training for Ministries programme, directed by a lay person. They have a packed church with a self-supporting teacher, and worker-priest, which leaves the rector and his wife free also to pastor several other more distant congregations. There is Bushbuckridge, busy quadrupling their church building, whose priest leader is a black hospital administrator recently ordained in a massive Assemblies of God church building to accommodate the vast throng from other churches in support of their minister. Nearby is Kabokweni, where the priest-in-charge is a police constable trained by Training for Ministries over six years, with several permanent deacons in training, trained and licensed to take communion to the sick and 'shut-ins'.

Robin Briggs said he could describe 'in almost every place, many small and struggling teams of self-supporting clergy, recently ordained, who work with volunteers and handful of stipendiary clergy to care for and grow the Church'. He briefly traced the influence there of the writings of Roland Allen, the Anglo-Catholic ex-missionary to China. Prophetically Allen had seen that the colonial Church – that required a vast élite of costly, stipendiary, professional, white expatriates to survive, let alone grow – would have to be radically transformed to become a self-supported, self-propagating, self-led Church reliant on the Holy Spirit, shaped by its treasures (the apostolic fundamentals, the Bible, creeds, sacramental patterns), and largely led by a reordered, locally based, volunteer, ordained ministry. Allen's vision gave impetus to the ministerial strategies of Bishop Wesley Frensdorff in Nevada, and is a deep influence now on the plans of the Diocese of Moray, Ross and Caithness, facing a similar economic climate, as well as other Churches in Britain (Bowden and West, 2000). Frensdorff's much-used meditation on the Church has become a litany of hope at many conferences dreaming of a Church 'so salty and yeasty that it really would be missed' (Borgeson and Wilson, 1990, p. 5).

Other influences, though more muted perhaps, included the French worker-priest movement in the Roman Catholic Church, and later, writers such as Leonardo Boff (South America) and Edward Schillebeeckx and Karl Rahner (Europe) and the unfulfilled model for a radical and sacramental Church contained in the documents of the Second Vatican Council.

Influenced by the powerful ideas of these writers and documents, when a parish priest near the mountains of Lesotho with 32 worship centres spread over a vast area, Briggs began preparing several local teachers for ordination, while others trained lay ministers to preach and pastor and to develop a centre to fight widespread malnutrition. Later in the Transkei, on the eastern seaboard, when Briggs was head of a provincial theological college in St John's Diocese, the diocesan bishop and synod supported the development of a college-based extension training programme, stretching into the remotest villages and aimed at raising up a huge team of volunteer clergy for the tiny spread-out village communities of the diocese, to be led and inspired by stipendiary clergy. Briggs described the continuing growth of this process.

In the Diocese of Pretoria, first as Director of Ministry Training and later as Suffragan Bishop, Robin Briggs worked to make a reality the dream he calls 'Every parish a school for ministry'. Basic to this dream has been the provision of formation and education for all – with a mandate to motivate, equip and enable the people of God to develop their gifts and give their lives in meaningful service. The Diocese of Pretoria has invested heavily in the programme to realize this vision and to make effective training and support available to all. The current Diocesan Bishop, Johannes Seoka, uses a version of Briggs's terminology when he refers to 'every parish a centre for Christian education'.

Robin Briggs used to commit every sixth Sunday to training lay ministers and ordinands who would travel enormous distances and sustain their studies over five or six years. Theological Education by Extension (TEE), using the resources of the Southern African TEE College, has the goal of raising up, training and ordering volunteer ministries of all the baptized as its major priority. In 1999 there were 150 students enrolled for a mixture of purposes. The paradigm shift that the Diocese of Pretoria has been seeking is rooted in the conviction that each local church must no longer be a priest-dominated, -led, -driven entity – but a community of communities, gathering weekly around word and sacrament, exercising mutual ministry and accountability. In Bishop Robin's experience, a parish will need at least seven years to make this shift. This resonates with my own experience of sowing seeds for the development of local ministry in the Diocese of Gloucester (see Greenwood, 1996).

The principles by which the Diocese of Pretoria has started to live include the following:

- Clear leadership from the bishop to move away from nostalgia for past days and to invest heavily in training volunteer laity and clergy.
- Belief in the gifts of the living God in a Spirit-fired sacramental Church that has a high expectation of all its members.
- Belief that people of all levels of trained intelligence have an effective contribution to make – and not just the graduate professional.
- Expectation that 're-treaded' stipendiary professional clergy have a vital role – as pillars, overseers, connectors, encouragers, trainers, humble team leaders, minibishops – overseeing three or more pastoral charges.
- The theological perception that baptism is at the centre of a co-ministering Church, rather than clerical hierarchies.

- Liturgical and catechetical expression of the Church as a company of volunteers.
- Diocesan provision of training and teaching, delivered locally, which is effective but inexpensive, in order to achieve a Church which is committed to being for all, for the poor.
- Belief in the power of the sacraments to convey amazing blessings to people when offered in the context of teaching and the power of the Spirit.
- Belief that every Christian community must have regular and convenient access to all the sacraments – baptism, anointing, communion – especially 'a full and glorious' celebration of the Lord's supper for all the Lord's people in that place on the Lord's day – lasting possibly for four hours.

Admitting that there are many practical issues and disappointments to face in a Church that chooses to change focus so dramatically, the bishop ends his account with the slogan 'Adapt – or die'. Early settlers including many Scots to his home area, the eastern Cape, in the 1820s found an area utterly unlike the promised land offered them by the Colonial Secretary. In his own words:

> hostile to agriculture as they knew it, violent – no welcome from the black groups living there that had had their land forcibly removed, which meant war; in many ways a living hell – but they had guts and foresight, and spiritual resources, to choose to adapt rather than to die in a foreign land .... Perhaps there is a lesson in all of this. 'Adapt – or die.'

I was moved and excited by Bishop Robin's vision and practice and describe them here as a lever for others to explore how they could be inspirational for renovating ministry in their own situation. There are also sharp questions, such as: How deep is the partnership here between diocese and local, bishop and congregation? Is the inspiration and methodology inherently hierarchical? If so, can such a model of authority possibly lead to a collaborative form of Church? Yet where inherited habits are to follow the lead of the clergy how does radical change occur effectively without being perceived as top-down? Who else but the bishop could 'give permission' for such a fundamental shift in the transcendentals of church life? What would happen if subsequent bishops in Pretoria were to hold completely different perspectives on ministry and mission? How far is this vision shared by the laity as a whole?

Since I first wrote this summary, I have had the benefit of a first-hand report from a colleague, Robert Paterson, Secretary of the Provincial

Council for Mission and Ministry in the Church in Wales, who visited the Diocese of Pretoria in February 2001. In his Charge to the Seventy-Ninth Session of the Diocesan Synod in June 2000, the new Bishop of Pretoria, Johannes Seoka – while expressing gratitude for the work of Bishops Kraft and Briggs, now retired – expressed the critical view that the emphasis on self-supporting ordinations had denigrated the ministry of the laity:

> Thus all of us want to be 'ordained' in order to serve God in his Church. Some who have taken holy orders should, in my opinion, have remained as dedicated laity. For example, some of our best lay people have become redundant or less active in ministry compared to when [sic] they were before they were ordained.

Although it must have been a blow to those self-supporting priests referred to in the speech, Bishop Johannes puts his finger on a serious tension in the present situation for Anglicans worldwide. Anglican Churches need priests living locally so that the Eucharist may be celebrated to support the whole Church in its daily mission. However, unless the role and task of clergy is redescribed and lived as a presiding work lifting all the laity through worship, encouragement and education into their rightful vocations, the ordaining of members of congregations locally will seem like a perpetuating of a Church rooted in clerical dependency. Bishop Johannes has begun a process of restructuring Training for Ministry and Spirituality but also encourages many local initiatives so that there can be a diocesan atmosphere in which 'clergy ... discover, encourage and develop the potential leadership of laity in their parochial units. I would like to see more lay leadership encouraged in our Diocese.'

There is always the temptation for the wealthier, better educated and more articulate (mainly white) self-supporting priests to feel less need for 'mentoring' and for those whose education, social standing, income and housing is poorer to feel very vulnerable. It is a huge task for arch-deacons, bishops and others who exercise diocesan leadership to challenge such divisions, teach that there are no permanent subordinations within Christian ministry, promote the definition of priesthood and the diaconate, and assist in creating adequate networks of mutual support and critique for new ministries.

Diocese of Newcastle, New South Wales, Australia

In his Charge to the 1996 Newcastle Diocesan Synod, Bishop Roger Herft offered the following analysis, based largely on research material provided to the diocesan council by the Hunter Valley Research Foundation in 1992:

> Australia as a society has moved from Christian and community values to a more secular and individualistic understanding of living. The statistics tell us that, as far as Church attendance goes, we have declined and that, of all the Church denominations, Anglicans have the most number of nominal members. Allegiance and loyalty, which were so much a part of previous generations, have gone. Young people seek other avenues to satisfy their spiritual yearning and the deep hunger for meaning. We have a choice. We can accept the decline, or we can decide to travel into the whirlwind of change, conscious that God is willing to be with us as we seek to be faithful to Christ's transforming ways.
>
> (Diocese of Newcastle, 1996)

Given the opportunity to take part in many Australian Anglican Church meetings and synods in the summer of 1999, I noticed that two presenting problems were very commonly spoken of – the need for more stable finances and for more young people. On one occasion in the Hunter Valley I recall the distress of older generations faced with young people who had 'changed' and with whom they had lost contact partly through their travelling long distances through each week to secondary school.

Evidence of a widening gap between the Anglican Church and the rest of the community was provided by the responses to the National Church Survey conducted in 1996 in Anglican and Protestant Churches throughout Australia. That survey pointed to the following characteristics of congregations within the Newcastle Diocese as compared with other denominations and with the general Australian population: a significant disparity between the age profile of Anglicans and that of the general population, the under-50 age group being considerably under-represented; a majority of attenders are long-term members and the percentage of newcomers is relatively low; a lower percentage of men and of members from non-English-speaking ethnic backgrounds; emphasis on traditional worship styles, a written liturgy and eucharistic worship; perception of little lay involvement in worship and only 29 per cent of lay people perceived themselves as having a teaching or administrative role; and an average clergy age of 51 years.

Annual parish returns further confirm this picture. These give evidence of ageing congregations, and difficulties in attracting and ministering to children and young people; problems of financial viability affecting both rural and urban parishes, limited financial and people resources necessitating the rationalization of clergy and property, and decreasing attendances in some areas. In the paper prepared for the Diocese of Newcastle in March 1999 by Philip Hughes of the Christian Research Association, the following conclusions were drawn:

> there are significant challenges throughout large sections of the Diocese, with higher levels than average of unemployment and low levels of skill. There are also many areas with young families. There may well be good opportunities for ministry here if the appropriate forms of ministry could be found.
>
> (Diocese of Newcastle, 1996)

Other perceived but unquantified factors that may be contributing to the widening gap between the culture of the Anglican Church in the Diocese of Newcastle and the surrounding culture include: a narrow parochialism on the part of some clergy and congregations in relation to the use of funds and resources and the demarcation of parish boundaries; a suspicion of diocesan 'interference' and centralism; clericalism in the understanding and practice of ministry; a hierarchy of order being assumed with clergy perceived as the 'real' ministers while the role of laity is to provide funds and support; traditionalism in worship and parish structures and a reluctance on the part of some congregations to consider alternative approaches; and the perception by some clergy that ordination implies a guarantee of lifetime 'employment' and that incumbency means tenure without external accountability.

The above picture conveys only part of the truth, and as with all generalizations is inevitably distorted. The diocese acknowledges the existence of a wide diversity of ministries seeking to respond to the diversity of conditions in the general community. It is further acknowledged that change and growth are occurring in numerous congregations, with the extent and pace of change varying considerably from place to place. The following is a brief summary of the process of thought to which the diocese felt itself to be called.

Theology of ministry

Believing that a review of ministry in the Church must begin from a re-examination of its theological foundations, the Diocese of Newcastle takes seriously the belief that to speak of mission is necessarily to speak first of the nature of God. From their understanding of God derives an understanding of ecclesiology, which in turn gives rise to an understanding of the character of Christian ministry.

A trinitarian faith

The Diocese of Newcastle believes that at the heart of Christian faith is God who is Trinity – three Persons unified in outflowing, mutual love, whose distinctive identities of Father, Son and Spirit are constituted in and through their relations with each other. The essence of God and of all Being is therefore relational. The created order flows from and mirrors the nature of God. Creation and humankind are relational in essence: to exist is to exist in relation. God who is Trinity of persons is the God whose being is other-focused and outward-directed, the God who is revealed as Creator, Redeemer and Sanctifier, a God of mission evidenced in the outflowing movement of creation, the movement towards humanity in Jesus Christ, and the sending of the Holy Spirit. The mission of God expressed in creation, redemption and sanctification is to bring the whole created order to the full realization of perfected interrelationship – the Kingdom of God.

The Church

The Newcastle diocesan policy statement goes on to express that this understanding of the nature of God requires an ecclesiology that is both relational in expression (mirroring the communion of the trinitarian relationship) and also eschatological in purpose (future-orientated towards the Kingdom). The Church called into existence by the triune God may be said to have the potential in Christ and through the Spirit to model or to be a sign of that communion which is the being of Godself and shape of God's desire for the ultimate ordering of the entire creation.

These fundamental characteristics are articulated in the various New Testament images of the Church such as: the Body of Christ, with its emphasis on organic growth, growth into Christ and continuation of the mission and ministry of Christ; the people of God, the new Israel called to live the covenant in the messianic age and to move ever onwards toward the fulfilment of the Kingdom; and spiritual household, the living temple of the presence of God built on Christ and 'filled, vivified, sustained and guided by the Spirit' (Küng, 1968). All these concepts express something of the nature of the Church as a single, yet diversified, incarnate spiritual reality originating in and mirroring, if imperfectly, the trinitarian nature of God, called into being through the power of the Spirit. The work of the Church can accordingly be expressed as worship, witness and service.

The Diocese of Newcastle distils these features to be echoed in the structures and functioning of the Church:

1 Unity in diversity, which should operate at all levels: local, diocesan, universal. This gives rise to the possibility of local variations within a wider framework of agreement, both at diocesan and ecumenical levels.
2 Relationships that mirror the trinitarian relationships of mutual, self-giving love, humility, contingency and the rejection of domination.
3 Authority originating from, authenticated by and exercised in the context of mutual relationship. Such authority is necessarily contingent.
4 Equality realized through difference. All are equally important but are endowed with different gifts and called to different functions.
5 A mode of existence and action that is incarnational, involved in the concrete reality of daily existence, and contextual, assuming different forms of expression in different cultural contexts.
6 An orientation both towards the past, the historical revelation of God in Christ, and towards the future, the *eschaton* and the full realization of the Kingdom.
7 Ecclesial forms and structures recognized as provisional and imperfect, since the Church is perpetually on pilgrimage, the goal of the Kingdom lying always ahead.
8 A cosmic scope of activity since the whole created order is the sphere of redemption. The focus of the Church is therefore both outward – into the world, the cosmos – and 'upward' – toward God.

Ministry

The Synod expresses its ministry in the Church, describing its task as part of the outworking of the mission of the Father realized in the redemptive work of Christ through the power of the Spirit, the vocation of all the baptized. Ministry encompasses three fundamental, interrelated elements: worship, witness and service. A local expression of the Church is defective unless it includes all three in dynamic balance. Baptism into Christ is the foundation of all Christian ministry and through baptism each follower of Christ is called into that ministry and given the gifts required to carry it out.

Through baptism, all are therefore called to participate in the total ministry of the Church, in accordance with their particular gifts and in the specific context of their life circumstances. Since the Church is made up of the baptized, its ministry is that of the whole people of God. A 1992 survey had found that the Church had created a world of super-apostles, the ordained, and a world of inferior apostles, the people. It concluded, 'We need to rediscover the true nature of people called by God' (Diocese of Newcastle, 1992, p. 74). Ministry is essentially a lay vocation to be exercised by the 'laos'; that is, the people. The Body of Christ image places particular emphasis on the interdependence and significance of the role of each member in the proper functioning of the whole. Ministry is thus a shared activity, to be carried on co-operatively in a co-ordinated way with various members exercising roles in accordance with their gifts, skills, calling of God and the requirements of the overall task.

The ordained ministry

The Diocese of Newcastle takes the view that ordination represents the Church's recognition and authorization of God's particular people to exercise specific roles within the larger and wider Church for the proper functioning of the whole. It does not function to 'set apart' (this is the function of baptism), but rather to 'set (certain people) within' the faith community for specific forms of service. Since New Testament times, formal authorization of certain ministries appears to have been given through the laying on of hands. While the New Testament Church had a diversity of authorized ministries, the three orders of bishop, priest and deacon gradually emerged as the predominant model, becoming by the end of the fourth century the universally recognized form of church order.

The diocese has found in *Total Ministry: Reclaiming the Ministry of all God's People*, by Bishop Stewart Zabriskie, an interpretation of the interrelated and differentiated functions of each of the three orders of ordained ministry with which it concurs. So the diocese concludes:

Bishops serve as symbols of unity
Bishops serve the fundamental unity through baptism of all members and local expressions of the Church. Their role is to function as shepherds, guarding and guiding the Church through leadership and teaching:

> It is the bishop's responsibility to provide that sense of spiritual direction that allows the people who are the diocese to maintain, stretch, and sometimes refocus the diocesan vision for ministry-to-mission, and in that revisioning to be accountable to one another in Christ.
>
> (Zabriskie, 1995, p. 38)

Priests act as a focal point for the local church community
They are set in the midst of the baptized to 'equip the saints for the work of ministry' (Eph. 4.12):

The priest gathers the community for its sacramental life, for the feeding and energizing that is central to the ministering community. The priest is the gatherer around the centre who is not the priest, but the Lord whom we all worship. The priest points the people toward the centre. The Church is a ministering community rather than a community gathered around a minister.

(Zabriskie, 1995, p. 48)

Deacons image the service and servant dimension of all ministry and focus the Church outward into the world
The function of the deacon is to encourage and help the ministering community for mission. They:

serve as postmasters, bringing in the mail (needs, concerns, hopes), sorting it out (helping to train some in the congregation for appropriate service and response), and sending it on (in dismissal for service).

(Zabriskie, 1995, p. 29)

These definitions make it clear that the ordained ministry is inseparably related to the ministry of the whole baptized community:

What (should) be emphasized is the symbolic connection of bishop, priest, deacon, and congregation in a partnership that ... expresses that fundamental unity through which each member of the body, through the gifts they have been given, is a source of empowerment to the others.

(Fenhagen, 1995, p. 70)

Implications for the functioning of the Church

The diocese believes that, in order to fulfil its calling, each local faith community will need to:

- further develop and nurture, through teaching, preaching, prayer and involvement, the understanding that ministry is the responsibility of all who are baptized;
- regularly and carefully assess its needs so that ministry that responds in an appropriate and effective way to the local situation can be developed. In some places this may necessitate a review of the current practice of locating a priest in every parish;

- provide training for laity so that they will be skilled in various ministries and witness within the Church and within society;
- encourage lay people to take responsibility for areas of nurture such as baptism and teaching and to exercise skills and expertise in administration, social issues and other areas of concern;
- support prayerfully and practically the ordained ministry in its task of preaching, teaching and sacramental ministry;
- encourage the clergy to practise a participatory style of leadership that shares and enables ministry with the laity;
- discover anew a holiness that is reflected in a servant role; and
- develop a team approach that extends beyond the local parish in order to facilitate the sharing of resources across the diocese.

A review of diocesan structures

The Diocese of Newcastle therefore recognizes that a theology of ministry that places emphasis on the interrelationship between bishop, clergy and people and on the necessity of developing partnership ministry at all levels calls for a review of the administrative structures currently in place. It has noted how the existing diocesan structures tend to be centralized and hierarchical. The major decision-making processes are shared by a relatively small number of people (senior staff, bishop's council, trustees of church property) and the same people are frequently to be found on diocesan committees. While over recent years there has been a deliberate attempt to broaden committee membership, ordinances determining composition of the decision-making bodies in the diocese preclude wider participation. The workloads carried by senior staff may be considered excessive. The majority of archdeacons, for instance, are required to provide priestly leadership of large parishes and supervision and oversight of assistants, and also to perform their archdiaconal duties across a large geographical region.

Existing structures are not perceived as adequately meeting the support, training and ministry development needs of either clergy or people. A radial structure is proposed to replace the existing hierarchical model. In this new model, the bishop is seen as being the centre of unity, the focal point from which radiates out all the ministry that occurs across the diocese. Responsibility for the development, support and administration of that ministry is shared by the archdeacons, each of whom has oversight of the various forms of ministry and ministering communities operating within a geographical region. The archdeacons would no longer have pastoral responsibility for a local faith community but might be attached to a local community on a part-time basis. Each of the functional entities located within a region (parishes, chaplaincies, aged care facilities, Samaritan programmes, schools, etc.) would have a direct link with the archdeacon and fall within their sphere of responsibility. It is further envisaged that this model would seek to strengthen cross-links among the various forms of ministering community within an archdeaconry, so that parishes, chaplaincies, schools, etc. develop collaborative ways of operating and provide mutual support and the shared use of resources.

Regional councils would become the decision-making and policy development bodies at the regional level, freeing the diocesan council to deal with matters relating to the overall functioning of the diocese. So there will be consequent changes in the roles of archdeacons, area deans, adult education and training and transitions between the ministries of stipendiary clergy.

Moving from the concept of 'parish' to 'ministering communities'

The Diocese of Newcastle asks, 'Is the parish dead?' At the beginning of the twenty-first century the local geographical area no longer forms the main location of community. Work groups, sports associations, service organizations and interest-based clubs have often replaced the 'village/parish' mentality where support for and by local activities was once paramount. Observation shows how far people in society will travel to take part in shared interest groups. Newer Christian denominations have capitalized on this by establishing worship and meeting centres where they can attract and accommodate members who often travel considerable distances.

The diocese recognizes that one of the key characteristics of the Anglican Church is its primary interest in maintaining a presence in every geographical locality as a basis, although even this concept can be built on by home groups and chaplaincies to retail outlets, large manufacturing premises, hospitals, prisons, residential homes or community centres. In such places many, who would otherwise have no contact with church, can find a place in a religious community. The Anglican Church has generally retained the traditional geographical parish model with buildings and faith communities in every town and suburb. In many areas the continuing viability of the existing parish model is questionable on account of limited financial and people resources. Land and building costs impede the establishment of new parishes in the growth areas of the diocese. Emotional, spiritual and financial investment in existing parish plant makes it difficult to let go of long-established worship centres.

It is nevertheless recognized that, in an increasingly fragmented culture, people have a fundamental need to experience community in some form. The signs are already beginning to emerge of Australians' desire to reconnect with each other, to re-establish a sense of belonging to a neighbourhood, a community, a society. Despite the obvious facts of greater mobility today, there is a deep significance for people in where their home is. The lack of human contact resulting from increased globalization and use of the Internet for communication leads to a renewed emphasis on the need to reconnect with each other, to re-establish a sense of belonging. Many church documents speak of 'community' as a goal for themselves as well as something they would be instrumental in fostering for all. Increasingly the theological foundation for this is purposefully to model or be a sign of the communion that is the being of Godself for the sake of the future of the world that is God's passionate desire. Local Ministry is an expression referring to the ways in which, increasingly, all Christians, because of their commitment to Christ expressed in baptism, are sharing that ministry that serves God's purposes through the whole Church in many differing ways. Since ministry is the baptismal vocation of the whole people of God, communities of faith are called to function as 'ministering communities'.

Defining ministering communities

When applied to the church context, the term 'ministering communities' in the Diocese of Newcastle (1996) means the following:

1 Communities are 'places or entities where each member can give something, where they can contribute something that they feel especially able to give, something that they are good at. The gift from each member is valued by the whole community and all gifts are unique and individual. The gift that a community gives back to each member is that of a role and connection.' 'Role' here is understood as an 'office holder' but in the sense of belonging to and holding a place in a community that helps to provide personal identity and meaning.

2 Such communities have an expectation of the mutual giving and receiving of everyone in their unique difference. Each finds identity and meaning in the interaction of each knowing their value and place. Bishop Wesley Frensdorff coined the expression 'ministering community' to distinguish it from Church as a community gathered around and dependent on an ordained minister. It is a Christian community of openness, belonging, mutual nurture and action, where everyone's ministry counts and is enabled to make a particular contribution to the life of the whole through the development of their gifts. Total or Local Ministry or building ministering communities is an

idea to live in as well as a group of people; it is a way of being the Church as well as an example of good practice; an idea to travel in as well as a map for the journey.

3   Total Ministry is rooted in the understanding of the Church as those called to minister. Ministering communities are lifelong learning communities in which people are continually transformed for ministry in God's mission. It is through life in community together that gifts are identified, called and used. Formation for ministry also requires community. A variety of ministry formation experiences should be made available for the diversity of need.

4   It is the responsibility of every ministering community to establish processes whereby those with a particular gift of ministry have that gift tested and affirmed for use, either within or beyond the fellowship of the Church. It is the responsibility of the local church, in partnership with the wider Church, the diocese; they ensure adequate and appropriate discernment, training, authorization and support for everyone called to exercise key ministry leadership responsibilities. This is of particular importance in the development of both authorized lay and ordained Local Ministry.

Conclusion

The ambitious practical expectation that every part of the life of the diocese is committed to outworking of collaboration as its key to mission and ministry will have implications for the selection and initial training of clergy, the fostering of a team approach in Local Ministry that in itself builds up all Christians in their vocation, raising questions such as 'Who should be leader in the ministering community?' and 'Can several churches work together as a ministry district?'

A major review was proposed, involving every possible group and avenue of enquiry and the use of visiting facilitators, leading to local three-year plans of action. The period of transition between the leaving of one stipendiary priest and the arrival of another is linked to the review process and involves the temporary ministry of an appointed 'transition priest' to provide sacramental and pastoral ministry as well as to facilitate the grieving and refocusing process. Unusually, the diocese treats the need and possibility of spotting potential conflict in advance, thus enabling conflict resolution to take place as a normal part of a healthy church. In this *kairos* time the diocese has plans for promoting the lifelong learning of all its accredited ministers and for equipping all the people of God engaged in mission. It is a bold and all-encompassing vision, rather than 'tinkering at the edges' as the Report (Diocese of Newcastle, 1996) itself notes.

I am grateful for the opportunity to have met with many of those involved in this process during my visit to Australia in 1999 and look forward to knowing more of the response of those members of congregations who are not part of synodical, wide-range planning, but who have traditionally simply 'gone to church'. What transformative patterns of education will be needed and will emerge? How will the bishops and archdeacons will manage the process when the vision catches on in one part of the diocese and not in another? What will be the timescale in rediscovering what will be the role of the priest within a 'ministering community'?

Diocese of Derby, England

'There has to be a better way of organizing the ministry of the Church than *merely* spreading clergy ever more thinly over the ground and lumping parishes together.' In 1998 the Council for Ministry (the group empowered by bishop and diocesan synod to provide leadership and resources for the formulation and development of the diocesan ministerial strategy) responded to that plea by offering the report *A Better Way* to the synod for consideration.

Before discussing what sort of ministry was going to be required, it was thought essential to come to an understanding of what sort of Church they perceived themselves to be at present, and what sort of Church God is calling them to become in the future. That is, first define the purpose and vision of the Church (for which there existed no such currently agreed and used definitions in this diocese), then decide upon an appropriate ministry which will help fulfil that purpose and realize that vision.

To that end, members of the Ministry Committee set out to listen to what God was saying both from within and from outside the Church. There was also a determination to hear what was being said at a local level. Therefore members asked an equal number of churchgoers and non-churchgoers in their parishes and workplaces how they perceived the Church. This was done by enquiring about their needs and expectations in relation to the Church, if any. The Council for Ministry's task was set against the background of a changing culture. Patterns of work, employment, voluntary activity and family life are elements in a society increasingly alienated from traditional religious practice and terminology. The research showed evidence of people asking the Church for help to make sense of their life experiences, and others looking for training and support that they might more effectively serve people in God's name. It was intended that this report would be a catalyst to enable discussion and action leading to the provision of appropriate ministry in every area of the county's life. As part of the listening process, prayerful attention was given to God's word in Holy Scripture and to church tradition.

All this research generated a great deal of data, which was initially processed in three intensive workshops by the Council for Ministry. At the final workshop it was decided that a committee of about 30 members was too large a group to allow further progress to be made. So the task was given to a small working group with a brief to produce a report which would seek to discern a diocesan strategy for ministry – ordained and lay, stipendiary and non-stipendiary – with a view to appropriate authorization and implementation.

That report was presented to the Council for Ministry in October 1997. After agreement had been reached the report was circulated as a consultation draft to incumbents, priests in charge, PCC secretaries and chairs of diocesan boards, councils and committees. The diocesan bishop, chairing the Council for Ministry, wrote an accompanying letter explaining the consultation process. This included the provision of five opportunities spread around the diocese at which the draft could be discussed with members of the working party. Over 200 people availed themselves of these opportunities. In addition, 69 written responses were received from individuals and representatives of some PCCs, boards, councils and committees, with seven responses being received from interested parties outside the diocese.

As a result of listening to all responses and suggestions for improvement, significant alterations were made to the consultation draft. The working group, on behalf of the Council for Ministry, submitted the revised draft to the Bishop's Council. After making minor amendments, the Bishop's Council submitted the report to be received and adopted by the diocesan synod in March 1998. The synod not only received and adopted the report by an overwhelming majority; it also requested that the proposals be considered and implemented by church councils, deanery synods and diocesan boards, councils and committees.

Proposed purpose for the diocese

In giving the report's proposals such a resounding endorsement, the synod announced the purpose for the diocese as 'To love and worship God in unity with other Christians offering witness and service to those communities in which we live and work'. But further questions were asked: 'What about God's particular call at this particular time?' 'What is God calling for in the future of this diocese?'

Proposed vision for the diocese

Having tried to hear what God was asking of the Church, the synod proclaimed its vision for the diocese as 'to be a Christian community recognized as experiencing and sharing God's salvation'. Theologically, the Diocese of Derby believes a Christian community is:

> recognized as such when it lives the life of God as a faithful, loving communion of people. We are made in the image of God who is Trinity. God is Father, Son and Holy Spirit, a communion of persons among whom there is a mutual equality but also distinction of identity and diversity of function. So should it be within the Christian community, not least in relation to mission and ministry.
>
> (Diocese of Derby, 1998)

The synod adopted words from the Roman Catholic Bishops' Report, *The Sign We Give*:

> The vocation of the Church is to be a communion, a living source of trinitarian relationships. That is the basis for our equality in dignity as members of the Church and for an awareness of the Spirit's activity within and between us. It is also the basis of the mission we share through baptism and confirmation. The Church ... is to be a sign and instrument of communion with God and of unity among all people.
>
> (Roman Catholic Bishops' report, 1995, p. 20)

The report continues:

> Just as Christians cannot talk about God revealed in Jesus except as Trinity, so we cannot talk about what God offers to us and calls us to offer to others, without talking about salvation (2 Tim. 1.9–10). To fulfil that purpose and realise that vision requires a renewed understanding of ministry. Because it is based on an early Church understanding of ministry there is nothing *new* in this strategy. It is more a case of renewing what already exists, but is perhaps hidden to a varying degree.

What is this ministry?

The Diocese of Derby expressed the belief that ministry is the outward expression of our inner Christian faith and discipleship. All faithful disciples have a ministry. It finds expression in a whole variety of ways depending on each person's particular gifts, commitments and life situation. It is as much to do with the place where we work, our home and family life, the interests we pursue, the organizations to which we belong, as it is to do with the place where we worship (1 Cor. 12; Eph. 4.7, 11–13). For most Christians most of the time, their ministry is going to be exercised where they live and work, not in church. For too long, the Church has tended to define ministry in 'church' terms, not in terms of the Kingdom of God. One of the greatest gifts the laity has to offer is making connections between what goes on in church and everyday life and work. The encouragement and releasing of this gift will transform the Church and our everyday ministry.

The diocese recalls that the Church is but a means to an end, not an end in itself. The end is God's Kingdom come on earth as in heaven. The Church is a means of helping to bring that about – and that is what is meant by mission. Mission means engaging with God's world as God's agents for his Kingdom. We are therefore called to be a mission-focused Church, a Kingdom-serving Church, not a Church absorbed by internal concerns. We are called to be a Christian community recognized as experiencing and sharing God's salvation.

The ministry of the baptized

For these profound theological reasons, the synod believed that a 'better way' to structure the Church's ministry is to base a strategy on the ministry of the baptized, and not just on the clergy. The diocesan synod therefore proposed a strategy for ministry based on the fundamental conviction that baptism marks the beginning of Christian discipleship, and all disciples are called to ministry. All ministry is a human response to the grace of God and is therefore the expression and visible out-working of that new relationship and calling to Christian discipleship. This conviction that the call to ministry begins at baptism, not ordina-tion, will come as a shock to many of the baptized. Maybe the shock would be lessened if they understood ministry as being the outward expression of an inner faith in their daily lives, as distinct from seeing ministry as the 'church bit' bolted on to the rest.

A further opportunity to discern and consolidate this ministry is provided by confirmation, at which point Christians personally commit themselves to the ministry God has given them. Confirmation preparation should therefore include an opportunity for those involved to reflect on the different ways Christians can live out their ministry. This opportunity is available in study courses such as Alpha, Emmaus, Credo and Education for Ministry. Along with confirmation, these could include a time for the discernment of particular gifts and opportunities for ministry that each candidate may have in their home, community, work, study or leisure as well as in their parish church activities.

The Report encouraged parishes to promote a culture where ministry review and renewal is available for every member on some regular basis; for example, on an annual Ministry Sunday. Every Christian has opportunities for ministry throughout their life, and these grow and change along with their faith and life circumstances; for example, in relation to age, marital status, employment, health. An annual review would help members reflect upon the effect of these changes in relation to their ministry.

Synod was invited to regard the laity as their greatest asset and resource. There were 20,823 baptized people on parish electoral rolls in the Diocese of Derby in October 1997. Even if that figure is reduced to the usual Sunday adult attendance of 17,648, it still represents an immense further potential for ministry. The ministry of the baptized – children, young people and adults – is about giving outward expression to an inner faith in their own particular life situation using their own gifts. The declared diocesan purpose sees that basic ministry as 'loving and worshipping God and offering witness and service to others'. So all the baptized are called to: love people by relating to them in a just and caring manner; worship and pray, both on their own and with others; witness by being able to explain what it is to be a Christian and how their faith relates to daily life; and serve by recognizing their own gifts of discipleship and then using these gifts for the benefit of others, especially those in need.

The diocese notes that as we are called to offer as God offers in Jesus, ministry will be painful at times. Like the exercise of God's grace, it can be a costly business. In terms of the needs of those we seek to serve in the name of Jesus, our research highlighted the importance of the following: offering a sense of personal meaning and direction in relation to God within a changing culture and communicating the Christian gospel in ways which people can actually understand; 'being there' for those in distress or trouble; offering friendship; taking children and young people seriously as full and integrated members of society and Church; allowing people just 'to be' in church; offering relevant opportunities for worship and spiritual growth.

The consequences that were identified in support of this fundamental ministry of the baptized were:

The ministry of the clergy
Ordination is described, with other accredited ministries, as a vocation to a particular ministry for which God calls and the Church selects, trains and deploys. For some that is a calling to stipendiary ministry, whereas

for others it is to a non-stipendiary ministry. For some time the Church has been reappraising the ministry of the ordained within the context of the ministry of the baptized. The reduction in the number of clergy and an increase of emphasis upon lay ministry, plus the rise in numbers and influence of Reader ministry, offer an exciting opportunity to undertake this reappraisal.

In the past there has been an assumption that the clergy, having been set apart for the purpose, 'do' the ministry on behalf of the Church and that the laity 'help' the clergy in their task. This (admittedly caricatured) understanding has been challenged in recent years by the rise of the concept and practice of 'every member', 'collaborative' or 'co-operative' ministry. Such ministry has clergy and lay people working together on a commonly agreed purpose, sharing the ministerial functions of the 'royal priesthood' among the communion of the baptized (1 Pet. 2.9).

The specific role of the clergy in this type of shared priesthood is to do at a local level what the bishop does at a diocesan level. That is, to exercise a servant leadership of caring oversight that will enable the priesthood of the baptized. For the laity to become more 'priestly' it is therefore necessary for the clergy to become more 'episcopal'. This understanding of the ministry of the clergy has a eucharistic dynamic in the Church; as a priest presides at the Eucharist at which others minister and all present participate, so the priest presides among the ministry of the local church.

The clergy are also called to be public representatives of God and the Church. This is also true of those lay people who are known to be 'church people' either at home or at work. But by virtue of their shared ministry with the bishop, the clergy represent the wider catholic Church. They speak and act on behalf of the Church and within the public perception are seen as those who have authority to proclaim the Word of God. Within Church and community they are also a focus of unity and reconciliation. This ensures diverse patterns of ministry are held together within the corporate purpose and vision. Because of their professional training, clergy are expected to possess a high degree of ministerial competence. This competence should be evident in their theological understanding and ability to preach and teach the faith, their conduct of public worship both of word and sacrament, their leadership within the Church and community, and their ability to offer care, confidential counsel and advice.

In summary, the diocese concludes that the range of contributions to the Church's life that clergy at various times are called to offer includes: representation, leadership, preaching, sacraments, unity and reconcilia-tion, theology, teaching, care, counsel and advice. It hastens to add that on the basis of the priesthood of the baptized it is anticipated that there will be others who are equally competent in the exercise of some of these ministries. However, the principal function of the clergy in relation to ministry is to enable the baptized to be the priestly people of God. In addition to the above competencies, this requires the acquisition and exercising not only of oversight, but also of insight to discern gifts of others, and of foresight to hold the vision before the whole people of God in that place.

As clergy, non-stipendiary ministers (NSMs) will also be involved in the process of enabling the baptized to be the priestly people of God, especially in those places where they live and work. NSMs – in particular, ministers in secular employment (MSEs) – are well placed to help fellow Christians make connections between faith, life and work, and to help interpret what Christian ministry means in that place. NSMs are also called to represent the Church to the world and the world to the Church. In this respect they model what all baptized and committed Christians are called to be and do.

The ministry of Readers

With their number in the diocese currently standing at approximately 260, there were seen to be more Readers in the diocese than clergy. The report suggests they have also been called by God to a particular ministry for which the Church selects, trains and deploys. It is a ministry of: leading worship; preaching; teaching; pastoral care; possibly officiating at funerals; and distributing the elements of Holy Communion.

The ministry of Readers is regarded by the diocese as serving as a model for the ministry of all the baptized, a ministry which is exercised in the community and the workplace as well as within structured life of the Church. Readers are licensed throughout the diocese. Although they usually relate to a particular congregation, it is of critical importance to the implementation of any strategy for ministry that Readers are selected, trained and deployed in a way that maximizes the use of their gifts for the benefit of the entire Church.

The collaborative ministry of the whole Church

Clergy and lay people together are therefore called to offer a ministry of salvation in the service of God's world. They do so as a communion of persons which, like the communion of the Holy Trinity, enjoys mutual equality but also distinction of identity and diversity of function. Mutual inequality or a blurring of identity and function between clergy and laity is therefore to be resisted. The diocesan synod sees that ministry of salvation being offered collaboratively in a number of ways, such as: worshipping God (word and sacrament); praying; promoting growth in faith understanding for all ages; discerning gifts of the Spirit; prophesying; engaging with the world (mission); proclaiming the gospel (evangelism); strengthening the unity of the Church; pastoring the healthy; pastoring the sick, the bereaved and others in need; and offering hospitality.

To support those ministries it is necessary to have other ministries of support and encouragement including: administration; finance management; property management; education and training; communication; co-ordination; and exercising oversight.

A strategy for Local Ministry

The vision that the synod proclaims for the diocese was one which would need to be worked through at the local level. In providing the ministries identified earlier – the collaborative ministry of the whole Church – the synod requested the development of Local Ministry throughout the diocese. The strategic implementation and development of Local Ministry was designed to ensure that the whole ministry of the whole Church is offered in that place ('place' refers to the parish and the places where people live out their ministry – at home, their place of employment or voluntary work and their place of leisure). How Local Ministry develops will depend upon each situation, but the PCC, with the priest, is to co-operate in promoting in the parish the whole mission of the Church, pastoral, evangelistic, social and ecumenical (see Church of England, Parochial Church Council (Powers) Measure, 1956).

The decision on how best to interpret the proposed diocesan purpose and vision, and how to establish Local Ministry, will be taken therefore at a local level. In striving to hold to the principle of working at a local level, individual parishes, team and group ministries, and local ecumenical partnerships (LEPs) will be encouraged to decide what is best for themselves. Different situations have different properties and call for different solutions. Therefore the basic question to be answered is, 'What form should Local Ministry take here?'

Once that question has been answered, the Report suggested, God will provide the necessary local resources, although it may be necessary to broaden what is understood by 'local'. Some parishes will have among their members enough people with the skills to organize all these ministries. Other parishes will need to co-operate across parish/denominational boundaries in providing these ministries.

The provision of these ministries may be co-ordinated in different ways:

- through the PCC itself, placing its task of promoting the whole mission of the Church at the centre of its work;

- through the PCC with the addition of people who have an expertise or interest in specific ministries;
- by the PCC setting up committees or working groups responsible for specific ministries;
- through a Local Ministry group set up by and accountable to the PCC; and
- by setting up a Local Ministry group relating to a number of parishes or churches of different denominations.

In working for Local Ministry, there is a fresh impetus to think ecumenically. Members of local churches meet with Christians from other denominations at work and socially. They are urged to recognize the potential for working closer together in these situations and in all church life.

It is hoped that, in inviting people to join in the provision of Local Ministry, PCCs will follow the example of Jesus and make improbable choices. Synod was told it is all too easy to choose those who already have jobs within the Church. Now look deliberately for others who are not so involved but have the following qualities: an enthusiasm for the particular ministry for which they are being invited to have a responsibility; enjoyment in working with others; being supportive of the gifts and callings of others; being committed to working to a common goal; able to listen and reflect; willing and able to negotiate and compromise; and with a passion to discern and help to release gifts in others. It is suggested that those responsible for specific ministries serve for a prescribed amount of time, to be decided locally.

Ordained ministers (stipendiary and non-stipendiary, MSEs), Readers, Church Army Officers, those in religious orders and stipendiary lay workers will work alongside those who organize Local Ministry. Some of them may be invited to take on responsibility for a particular ministry, but they must facilitate and not monopolize the Local Ministry of the baptized, nor compromise Jesus' choice of improbables. The parish priest's main function in relation to Local Ministry is seen as in exercising, caring and encouraging oversight; with the PCC, faithfulness to the gospel of salvation.

Implementation
Some parishes will recognize the model of Local Ministry being proposed because they are already doing it; that is, the ordained are already exercising a ministry of oversight in relation to an extensive ministry of the baptized. Other parishes struggle to survive because the number in their congregation is small and the average age is high. This inevitably

results in a few individuals becoming even more tired as they carry an undue load of ministerial responsibility.

Local Ministry offers a strategy for ministry that shares burdens and spreads the load. The report acknowledges that some lay people will be able to give more than others and this will change as life circumstances change. It also acknowledges the importance of hard-pressed laity being able to 'rest in the Church' in order to exercise their ministry of discipleship. We need to receive the ministry of others as well as to exercise our own.

Weariness may be caused because some local congregations are trying to do too much. There are just too many services and perhaps too many buildings to maintain. The implementation of Local Ministry could provide an opportunity for undertaking a review of worship and buildings, not least in consultation with other churches nearby of a different denomination. This would be a review set within the context of becoming a more mission-orientated Church, less dominated by maintenance.

There are different ways of working within deaneries and across parish and ecumenical boundaries. This will depend on the local situation and its needs. One example is a shared youth or community worker. The absence of young people from the congregations of many churches is a matter of deep concern. A significant number of individual parishes feel helpless in the face of this absence. But the joint appointment of a youth or community worker to work across a number of parishes or churches would make a major contribution towards addressing this concern.

Another example of a ministry shared among parishes is administration. Imagine the benefit of one person, a gifted and skilled administrator, exercising that ministry on behalf of a number of parishes. This would liberate a consequent number of 'reluctant' administrators for ministries more in line with their own particular vocational gifts and skills. Shared administration also raises the possibility of sharing the ministries of managing finance and property, although that would entail a high degree of trust and respect between parishes. But again, the benefits could be considerable. Other possibilities for sharing ministries across parish boundaries include teaching (especially certain age groups) and evangelism (not every parish has an evangelist).

In relation to finance, the generally understood policy of the diocese is that parishes are individually responsible for church buildings and corporately responsible, through the bishop and parish share, for ministry. It may be necessary for that corporate responsibility to be extended through the budget to resource the initial training for and development of Local Ministry. There may also be a need to support wider continuing ministerial education, but the administrative costs of parish work should continue to be borne locally. The implications of full- or part-time stipendiary lay appointments will require careful consideration. Groups of parishes or churches of different denominations may decide that they can finance a particular appointment. This is happening in some parishes now. When such an appointment strengthens Local Ministry, these developments are encouraged.

There may be some appointments that are so wide-ranging or meeting a specific need in particular area that it seems appropriate to fund them from the diocesan budget. Before such decisions are made, there are many factors to be considered. The diocesan pastoral committee will have to consider carefully the argument for a lay appointment and the diocesan board of finance assess the implications on the budget and consequently the parish share. The report recognized that the Diocesan Local Ministry Steering Group works closely with the diocesan pastoral committee and board of finance to establish a procedure for considering all new initiatives in response to the development of Local Ministry that seek financing through the diocesan budget.

The Diocese of Derby believes it doesn't have a problem of supply of ministers, only a problem of organization. All of these ministerial resources need to be harnessed in response to local self-perceived needs. Those are the needs that have to be met in order for Local Ministry to help realize the diocesan vision in that place. What must be strongly resisted is using clergy and Readers in ways that prevent the realization of that vision. This would happen if clergy and Readers were to operate in a manner to provide a pattern of ministry that encourages reliance on licensed ministry at the expense of the ministry of others. The temptation to fall back into old patterns of ministry is considerable. The synod is invited to accept that the vision God holds out can be realized only if as a mission-focused Church there is a policy and strategy for ministry based on the Local Ministry of all the baptized.

For that reason the synod was not at this stage recommending the introduction of ordained Local Ministry to the diocese, until the real energy of Local Ministry among the laity, Readers and existing clergy has become established. The Synod attended to detailed issues about the authorizing and commissioning of Local Ministry teams, Readers and clergy to better effect a partnership of shared authority among all ministers, ordained and lay.

In 1998 the diocese appointed a parish development/mission adviser specifically to spearhead the implementation of *A Better Way*. Initially he found that although the diocese had asked itself strategic questions, on the whole local churches had not. In this role Barrie Guage found himself needing to offer education and training to around 1,000 parishioners at different centres on issues such as discerning gifts, practical ministry and community involvement. Although there was some resistance – summed up in one vicar's cry from the heart, 'Just leave us alone!' – Barrie was able to write in February 2001, 'There are now small signs of movement in the light of *A Better Way*.' Clergy training days have been instrumental in 'creating a mechanism for collaborative discernment'.

So although in Barrie's view *A Better Way* remains largely a prophetic document, further hampered by the need to increase revenue, I find this exercise to which the Diocese of Derby has given so much time an exemplary process of dialogue, with real potential to lead to the welcoming by many parishes and clergy of its vision and strategy. I am aware of a significant number of articulate voices who would be concerned that such a strategy denies a significant element in the traditional expectation of congregations and general public of the ordained. Personally I find the main conclusions and the process of reaching those conclusions extremely congruent with the ethos and basic condition for Church inspired by the New Testament, and by the insights into the dynamic of God's patterns for living in hope shown in Jesus and the work of the Spirit to renew ecclesial structures now.

Diocese of Northern Michigan, USA

This is a description of a much more closely framed and episcopally led scheme for changing the paradigm of the Church's ministry. Northern Michigan – the Upper Peninsula of Michigan – is 300 miles wide, 200 miles from north to south, and has a population of 300,000 – and a higher number of deer. The people who live there are affectionately known as 'Yoopers'. The Upper Peninsula of Michigan is remote and has extreme weather conditions. There are long, cold winters with hundreds of inches of snow. The area is heavily wooded, with few scattered towns and villages with tiny populations and a struggling economy. Among the small scattered churches of Northern Michigan, inspired initially by Bishop Tom Ray and now by Bishop Jim Kelsey, the conventional ministerial pattern of each parish having a priest has become untenable and required the discovery of alternative sustainable models. Indeed a bold experiment in replacing traditional ministry with 'a plan for mutual ministry' has been running now for two decades. One account speaks of a lens being ground in Northern Michigan that could throw critical questions – about church structure and the very nature of priesthood – into new and sharper focus. 'Out of the praxis of communities which were oppressed within the Church, a theology of ministerial liberation is emerging' (Arbogast, 1994, p. 8).

The Northern Michigan ministry plan speaks of showing Christ to the world through the life of the Church – its worship, mutual care, and learning; and its mission of reconciliation, servanthood and proclamation. Total Ministry is defined by the diocese as 'the building up of the local community so that all its members recognize and offer their gifts in ministry both corporately and individually, both within the Church and in the wider community'. Like Pretoria, building on the theology of Roland Allen and principles drawn from Paul's theology, there is a deliberate move away from a Church in which the primary minister is the ordained 'professional provider', who may choose helpers as a ministering team. As Bishop Tom exclaims, 'When we say 'vacancy' – as the time between the leaving and the arrival of stipendiary clergy – do we mean there's nobody there?' The diocese, taking seriously a trinitarian doctrine of creation, assumes that the interrelations of daily life are the main arena for ministry. Following the radical equality of the life of Jesus and the disciples (Mark 10.28–31), the diocese assumes that every baptized person, according to their gifts, shares actively in Christ's ministry. A briefing pamphlet proclaims:

At Eucharist, we gather as a community of radical equality, gathering to be with the resurrected One, to embrace and to be embraced by God's Holy Spirit. We do this because Yahweh will not be Yahweh alone. And because the Church itself is called to be a sacrament of interrelatedness.

In transforming congregations into ministering communities, there is a clear message that ministry is delivered neither by clergy nor by ministry teams. Following the spirit of Paul's approach, they are working towards clusters of ministering communities engaging the ministry of all the baptized, developed by Local Ministry support teams.

Through a covenant group process, the bishop (or a representative) meets with the local vestry to present the possibility of refocusing the daily life and mission of that congregation. If the local leadership decide to proceed, the bishop (or representative) visits to preach and, with members of the vestry, to lead a full presentation regarding the possibility to the full congregation. If the consensus is to proceed, a consultant is selected who will be with the congregation throughout the process.

To avoid any sense of undue haste, the consultant leads a series of at least four meetings attended by members of the vestry and any other leaders identified by them. The full membership list of the congregation is reviewed for various roles on the ministry support team. No individual is identified for more than two positions. Those identified for these roles are invited to covenant for a period of preparation. All members of the congregation are invited to join this covenant group as members-at-large. The covenant group meets twice a month for three- to four-hour sessions, with the consultant attending almost every session. These meetings are shaped by the curriculum that has been prepared by the diocesan team of consultants. It is anticipated that it will take between 18 and 24 months for the curriculum to be completed. In addition to these bi-weekly sessions, there are periodic diocese-wide workshops for those preparing for various roles in their ministry support team. Upon completion of the curriculum, the members of the covenant group are examined together by the commission on ministry.

Following this preparation, and all necessary approvals by the bishop, the standing committee, and the commission on ministry, the ministry support team is designed to the needs of that particular local church and commissioned at a liturgy during which the ministry of all the baptized is affirmed and those who will serve on the team are duly ordained and licensed.

The ministry support teams are made up of a circle of those with diaconal, apostolic and priestly ministries. The diocesan briefing paper explains:

> Today it is Sarah's circle, not Jacob's ladder that must serve as our paradigm. Just as in medical education the paradigm has shifted from a lecturer with a pointer and a skeleton to students and their mentor sitting together in a circle – and in that circle, too, the person seeking medical attention! To be with and to be for, that's the heart of ministry.

Deacons teach and engage in social-justice matters; the need and shape for this work are identified and co-ordinated by diaconal ministry co-ordinators. Apostolic ministries include those who co-ordinate stewardship of gifts and money, leaders of educational programmes, ecumenical co-operation, and the work of consultancy and supervision. The priestly ministry includes the priest who exclusively presides at and administers sacramental worship, the preachers, and those involved in planning, educating for and leading worship.

There is in this diocese a fluid energy when everyone takes joint responsibility in their differing ministries for being the Church. The emphasis is on the way a team supports the ministry of the whole so that clerical dependency is not accidentally reinvented. Ordained local ministers are not there to have placed on their shoulders all that once was inappropriately expected of clergy who had been trained residentially. The ordained are asked at the commissioning of the team, 'Will you support these people in their ministries?' Budgets are not over-weighted by the costs of paying clergy, leaving more money for the development of the mission of all.

Even though some churches will see this as attractive for financial reasons, Bishop Tom Ray passionately expresses his view that God's Spirit is dragging them relentlessly, inexorably to see another map emerging. This is why the diocese as a whole needs to model precisely the mutual ministry looked for locally. Total ministry is not based on the idea that some are ordained to do what no one else in the congregation can do:

> My God, that's seductive! And dangerous. The larger you draw the circle for the ordained person, the more destructive. Liturgist, administrator, preacher, teacher, pastor, intervenor, visitor, community leader, brings in the youth. What's left outside this very intimidating circle? Not much. This is a recipe for paralysis and impotence, for separation, for clericalism and anti-clericalism. This recipe guarantees for clergy that they will be isolated in that circle, overworked, unsupported, and broken. We break clergy constantly, and clergy families are in deep trouble. This recipe guarantees for the laity that they will be underutilized, undervalued, have low self-esteem; and they will be disappointed in the clergy eventually.
>
> (Ray, quoted in Arbogast, 1994)

Those who were able to witness from their own experience of total ministry at the 1999 San Francisco symposium spoke about a revolution in understanding ministry as for all and, throughout the week, an excitement about learning, social responsibility and prayer. As one speaker said, 'The difference is like saying to a mountain, cast yourself into the sea, and have it obey!' From the total ministry movement in the Diocese of Olympia came the comment, 'Total ministry is not a cookie cutter program: as the congregations enter more deeply into the commitment of conversion, there is an accompanying deepening of spirituality and dedication to prayer and to corporate discernment.'

In Northern Michigan over half of the congregations of the diocese have entered a covenant process by which members of their community are being identified and studying together as a ministry support team to honour the baptism of all. So this model is very clear, boundaried and episcopally led. There are clearly experiences of liberation and the free flowing of the energy of many church members finding new possibilities of ministry, education, confidence and conversion.

Again it has been the bishops who have been boldly instrumental in breaking with inherited ministerial patterns – through their knowledge of theology, willingness to teach it and turn it into workable strategy, defend decisions with rigour and hold the consistency. What would have happened, I wonder, had the bishops been confidently advocating an authoritarian, top-down ministry plan? Rather, light is shed on the role of the bishop as one who sees the global picture and can read the signs of the time and help others to do the same. The implicit extension of traditional ministries of overseeing, priesthood and serving to a wider team of commissioned laity may cause some confusion and require more work on seeing how each in their particular though mutual ministries has something distinctive to contribute. But in moving out of the paradigm of ministry almost entirely displaced by the clergy, it seems inevitable that there will be differing views and experiments requiring a continuous process of sifting, rather than a holding back until everyone speaks the same language or holds an identical vision.

Diocese of Chelmsford, England

Sometimes small beginnings in one part of a diocese become a critical mass, so releasing new energy more widely. In my work in the Diocese of Chelmsford, the principles of Local Ministry were publicly accepted and promoted by the bishops and debated at synods, under the banner of 'ministry as partnership'. Many parishes and clergy had for years practised varying forms of the ministry of all the baptized but the prevailing culture was still one of clerical dependency at a time when our ability to sustain it was rapidly disappearing. The signs that God was calling us to move to a new set of paradigms of Church (taking account of differing spiritualities and theological languages) went largely unacknowledged until the bishop's council acknowledged we were increasingly under pressure through shortage of money and resources. Then – in the spirit of Roland Allen that you use the resources you have rather than yearn for the ones you would have liked – a few pioneering spirits led the way, recognizing the way was not to have a detailed prescriptive scheme for developing Local Ministry. Rather, the diocesan synod concluded that the way forward was to have a few basic principles undergirding a strategy for Local Ministry to become simply the normal way we were Church in the everyday routines of ministry in mission, differing in many contexts – and that this transition would take a long time to achieve.

There was no intention at this stage to invite vocations to ordained local ministry (OLM) but to concentrate instead on building up ministry leadership teams of existing clergy, Readers and laity chosen by the PCC. Three years later, responding to strong concern among some of the area deans, a working group was set up by the bishop to examine the question of OLM. At this stage its recommendation to experiment with an 'OLM-like' ministry has yet to be considered by the synod. The primary recommendation is that:

the Diocese should experiment with an OLM-like Ministry in six

Ministry Teams – preferably two from each Episcopal Area. The purpose of this experiment should be to explore the potential of OLM for ministry and mission, and to determine whether a full OLM Scheme or alternatively, modifications to the present NSM Scheme, would be appropriate here.

(Diocese of Chelmsford, 2000)

There was a determination in the group not to damage the potential development of ministry leadership teams by rushing quickly into filling gaps with more priests even though, paradoxically, priesthood reinterpreted is a vital element in building up the whole body of Christ and in particular the ministry teams that can focus new expectations of ministry as partnership.

What in practice triggered the energy flow was a sudden request from one of the parishes in east London to the area bishop to license their ministry leadership team. 'What do I do now?' e-mails the bishop. Shirley Cutbush, a laboratory manager and lay chair of Newham, a staunch advocate and proactive worker for the development of ministry leadership teams, takes up the story in her own words.

At our previous Diocesan Ministry as Partnership (MAP) meeting we had decided to ask the bishops this very question. We needed to know what criteria they would be looking for and how to progress with almost zero resources. The parish request resulted in the rapid formation of the West Ham Archdeaconry Local Ministry Group (WHALM). After three meetings and discussion with the bishops there emerged seven basic guidelines which have become clearer through further discussion.

(For the Second Diocesan Local Ministry
Conference, October 2000)

Ray Armstead, a member of a ministry leadership team in east London, a facilitator in a different parish, and a member of WHALM, temporarily wrote up the bishops' commissioning principles in the form that follows. As part of the negotiation process between a bishop and a parish requesting that they be acknowledged as having a commissioned ministry leadership team, the following seven conditions apply. In one way or another there has to be evidence of all of these.

A PCC resolution to establish a ministry leadership team (MLT)

Total ownership of the ministry leadership team (or preferred local wording; for example, ministry support team) is crucial to its success.

Therefore both PCC and congregation must be enthusiastic for and aware of what a MLT will mean to them. In order to meet this need, it may be helpful to accept consultancy from a minister from a neighbouring church (for example, by inviting a speaker to talk on 'ministry as partnership' (MAP), to the whole church). Part of the diocesan provision is *Ministry as Partnership*, a study guide to be used in groups. The recommendation is that the local church (however defined) engage for as long as necessary with the MAP resource book and other materials as a vital part of growing together in their views, as a ministering community, on the value of a 'Local Ministry' approach to 'doing Church'. After consultation with the congregation the PCC should write a clear resolution to establish a MLT and then vote on that resolution. If proper preparation has taken place the vote will be clear.

An agreed constitution, which describes the relationship between the PCC and the MLT

The MLT is not in competition with the PCC. The PCC are and remain the elected representatives of the congregation, responsible with the parish priest for holding and developing the vision for mission in that place. However, the PCC has a vital role in supporting the development of Local Ministry. The PCC needs to oversee the purpose, shaping, setting up, well-being and nurture of the MLT, receiving regular reports and making relevant enquiries in order to support the MLT, both physically and spiritually.

Some form of consultation, facilitation and appraisal

Consultation may form part of the initial process of talking to the PCC, opening up the possibilities of *Ministry as Partnership* and helping to ensure that discussions involve as many people as possible. Facilitation should be undertaken, preferably by a pair working together to strengthen the self-awareness of the MLT and to help all its members to find an appropriate voice. Appraisal is important to keep the team healthy; it will ensure MLTs are functioning as teams and paying due regard to their spiritual life, and will highlight any training needs.

A working agreement for team members

The working agreement will be between the PCC including the priest and the those individual ministry team members who at any one time comprise the MLT. A working agreement will clearly outline what can be expected from both parties; for example, the total number of hours a week the person can comfortably manage, given their other responsibilities, and any training that the individual feels they need. It will also state the commitment that the PCC gives to the team member financially – perhaps a budget or out-of-pocket expenses – through prayer and regular review.

Initial and continuing training

Facilitation will form part of this training but other forms of training and learning will be appropriate either for individuals or the team as a whole. As well as training to encourage the specific spiritual gift of the individual, training may be useful for the whole group to enable them to gel and act as a team and for the team to learn how to become educators and enablers of the entire congregation, constantly looking for and building up the spiritual gifts in their church. Clergy and Readers on the MLT, as well as laity with all their various educational experiences, will hopefully learn from each other in reflecting on God's work in the spheres of all their ministries.

A commissioning service for the parish

This is the public declaration by the diocese that the parish now has a ministry leadership team that has been well prepared for and every likelihood of remaining healthy and effective. The team's membership will continue to evolve over months and years. The commissioning will be led by the bishop or the archdeacon and will provide a 'shop front' for everyone to see that the way of being 'Church' is in the process of change. As many local people as possible should be invited to attend; for example, invitations could be extended to the local police, hospital staff, fire brigade personnel, local councillor and mayor. This will help people to understand why in future accredited visitors from the 'church' may not be wearing a clerical collar. The commissioning is of the parish having a MLT, rather than encouraging individuals themselves or the congregation to believe they have joined the ranks of the 'hierarchy'.

As a permanent mark of the occasion, the bishop issues to the parish a diocesan certificate inaugurating the ministry leadership team. This offers the promise of episcopal support, a long-term commitment when appointing subsequent clergy and the expectation of regular review.

Attendance at the annual diocesan local ministry conference is required of MLTs

This is for the sharing of local good practice with that of others in different contexts and to promote the culture of a learning Church that listens to its context and in so doing changes both itself and that context.

Time and experience will inevitably mean the adaptation of these working principles, but they offer sufficient shape and allow for spontaneity for the present. The number of parishes throughout the diocese commissioned by area bishops as having a team is slowly increasing. The energy of the West Ham Archdeaconry Local Ministry committee is being further developed by the involvement of Building Bridges of Hope (BBH – part of Churches Together in Britain and Ireland especially concerned with learning how to be mission Churches). The occasional presence of a participant observer from BBH is intended to be a non-directive listening support to further encourage local enthusiasm and autonomy in mission.

Shirley Cutbush, Co-ordinator of WHALM, well summarizes the current situation:

> We know there is a lot of lay ministry already happening in many Churches, but without a proper framework it can easily disintegrate. People suffer burnout, new incumbents come with new ideas, bad practice develops without proper education or training. As a volunteer with a day job I am careful to call myself a co-ordinator, a communication point for parishes. I can put them in touch with whatever help, support or advice they need. I can envisage this will be of the peer support variety, keeping a parental eye to make sure things are going in the right direction rather than holding hands all the way. This should be a good model to follow if we want to demonstrate Ministry as Partnership in practice. I truly believe that the future of the Church of England lies with Ministry as Partnership. However, our long history of paternalistic styles of ministry means that the energy presently lying dormant in parishes can only in reality be released with the 'permission' of those at the lectern.

Final Reflection

Throughout much of the world now, in varying contexts, in a huge variety of vocabularies, spellings, technical phrases, and theological perspectives, the phenomenon exists of carefully planned partnership in ministry for mission. For those in the centre of it, there hardly seems any surprise or point in talking about it: 'This is simply how we do Church here now.' Many further illustrations could have been given from Britain, Canada, Australia and New Zealand. Yet there is obvious pride and a real sense of having come through many trials in those who stand up at conferences to speak up with passion for radical equality in ministry as a necessary and rudimentary condition for being – or doing – Church. But the gifts of tenacity, clarity and endurance are needed in abundance to persuade dioceses to act coherently and congregations to let go of the dominant paradigm of Church with which we have lived for too long.

I frequently hear the comment that we have recruited, trained and deployed clergy to serve in a parish for decades and still there are so few signs of the laity being emboldened or developed. In fact statistics show how many laity are simply walking away from church membership – which is not the same as having no belief in God. If Churches are prepared to learn from society, we can identify many experiments in businesses, schools, and the police and armed forces. A recent article in the *Harvard Business Review*, for example, demonstrates how experimenting with being captain of a ship in a different way – including crucially his own attitude – allowed in the crew of *USS Benfold* the combination of a sense of corporate endeavour and individual affirmation to achieve the goals of combat readiness, personnel retention and trust. Through receiving high-quality attention, coaching and obvious trust in their capabilities, as well as clear operational boundaries, from the captain, the crew became more highly motivated (see Abrashoff, 2001). I am indebted to Tony Chesterman's reflection on this risky way of being captain as a sign of God's unconditional and attractive love.

> In Jesus this unconditional love offers a way back to God, i.e. it redeems people by offering them the vision and values of a different way of being human. So we have a different way of being captain, a different way of being crew, a different way of being God and a different way of being human.
>
> (Chesterman, unpublished letter, 2001)

It has been a recurrent theme of this book that collaborative ministry in the Church is more than a better way of getting things done at a time of financial and clergy recruitment shortage. The way we choose to be Church is for the growing up in wholeness of all who take part and as a sign to the world of a better way. In this period between Easter and the coming of Christ in glory, we have also to recognize that many of God's promptings will come to the Church from unexpected sources.

The renaissance of a relational doctrine of the Trinity has the tools to permit a fundamental critique of hierarchy. Catherine LaCugna painstakingly traces recent developments in patterns of trinitarian thought in the light of a feminist critique. She uses the concept coined by the Greek Fathers of *perichoresis* (and already mentioned) to describe the unity of the divine persons as mutually inherent in one another, drawing life from one another, being what they are by relation to one another. So she writes:

Perichoresis means being-in-one-another, permeation without confusion. No person exists by him/herself or is referred to him/herself;
this would produce number and therefore division within God.
Rather, to be a divine person is to be *by nature* in relation to other
persons. Each divine person is irresistibly drawn to the other, taking
his/her existence from the other, containing the other in him/
herself, while at the same time pouring self out into the other.

(LaCugna, 1992, p. 271)

There is no room for a hierarchy of importance among ministers here: 'It
will not be so among you' (Matt. 20.26; and see Matt. 18). Yet lest we get
carried away completely by the eloquence of dynamic theological prose,
we had better recognize that paradigm shifts take a huge period of
persuasive debate and time and that every generation of Christians has
lived with many different models of Church in coexistence. Nevertheless
as we live out of our ideas, they had better be ones most able to enable
our Church to live out God's trinitarian life for the sake of the world.

A trinitarian interweaving of *koinonia* – as communion, community
and communication of Christ's presence in the world – erodes the
polarizations that once we took for granted. Total ministry will tolerate
no false dichotomy between church or world, laity or clergy, mission or
ministry, faith or practice, proclamation or dialogue, worship or human
responsibility, children or adults. As the undertow of conservatism is so
strong, pulling us back into familiar clerical dependency, in all forms of
leadership we shall need particular wisdom of two kinds. One is that of
watchfulness. A bishop in an English diocese who regularly has breakfast
with the diocesan Local Ministry staff team memorably asked them to
keep a watch on him. 'When you see me or hear me slipping unconsciously into old ways and language, or making staffing appointments
that are discordant with our strategy, pull me up and remind me of our
new vision and plans.' I find this a powerful picture but I also want
bishops who will watch out for themselves because they recognize what
is at stake. But just because we ordain a few people as bishop does not let
everyone else off the hook – no one in the baptized and baptizing
community is called to irresponsibility. The bishop at breakfast with
the team reminds us all – in our particular place in the Church – to be
watchful and to support one another in resolving to create a Church of
equal and different ministers, through our choice of language, symbolic
action, and the apparently trivial decision or remark.

The second area where we need wisdom is more subtle. We have seen
in this chapter how some dioceses are very directive while others lay out
principles, giving freedom to local churches to respond. Discerning when
to apply pressure and when to leave room for choice, when to let things

find their own pace and when to urge people to new possibilities is a question of how we understand authority and how we respect the spiritual maturity of all. The method by which a diocese will introduce Total, Mutual or Local Ministry in a particular place and time is itself precisely about the identity of the Church. I believe the energy is already present in the community of all the baptized – the Spirit blowing where it will – but the unlocking of visions inevitably will depend on the processes encouraged by those in positions of ordained and accredited authority. Those with responsibility for overseeing the local church – whether in the centre of a city, a school or prison, or in a wide rural territory of several church centres – have the primary responsibility to assist the Church as a whole to the widest possible vision, and each of the members together to know God's calling and to encourage and find support for its lively fulfilment. Andrew Bowden and Michael West have painstakingly documented some of the problems that emerge when the picture is too small and when individual ministers, lay and ordained, act in isolation or as though they do not understand their particular and interrelated contribution (Bowden and West, 2000).

One of the consistent arguments of this book is that to promote an ordered spontaneity, moving away from inherited and stifling patterns of benign hierarchy is an important task. It means that the relation between the global and the local church cannot be assumed as top-down, nor can it just be left to chance. If the latent energy of local churches, arising out of the generous blessings of God's provision, is to be creatively engaged, then some security and 'parenting', including much freedom to explore, need to be available. Local Ministry is a key way of talking about the Church's need to discover coherent, sustainable patterns for mission and ministry at the present time. Reflecting on practice recorded in this chapter and in many parts of the world, I believe every diocese has a responsibility to set in its midst a group with respected authority to contemplate such questions as the following:

1 How does change happen in structures of ministry? What is the particular contribution of bishops and archdeacons? How do we provide a safe enough and yet free arena for experiment?

2 It seems faintly ridiculous for a bishop or priest to declare, 'I've decided that from tomorrow, we've all going to be collaborative.' But how does change happen in conditions of residual resistance? What are the appropriate points of intervention? How does Local Ministry become more than 'Let's help the overworked vicar'? How do we lovingly but with resolve challenge the habits of the overworking archdeacon and bishop? Surely their inappropriate modelling makes

genuine change to a learning, collaborative, partnership in ministry almost impossible.

3 How much variety of practice can a diocese accommodate? How do bishops, archdeacons and diocesan advisers approach situations in parish 'teams' that seem to be set up on principles far from those espoused in diocesan strategy documents or that would be impossible to sustain with the arrival of a new vicar? If a prevailing pattern seems right to synods and a huge majority of church members, what energy is left for supporting and critiquing other practices? What is the compromise solution between variety and uniformity?

4 There are serious questions about the relationship between the tasks and responsibilities of wardens, PCCs, synods and ministry teams. What role could a deanery standing committee have? How will ecumenical and other local combinations of Churches be authorized, supervised and appraised?

5 What is the diocesan belief about the value of a Local Ministry team? Is it an expanded substitute for the traditional vicar role or a catalyst for the ministry of the whole community? Is 'ministry' the word best used for the gifting and calling of some Christians or does Local Ministry rest on a belief in 'every member ministry'? Where is the Reader in all this? Who is providing the necessary education and training, to allow for ministers on the ground to think hard about such questions?

6 In discerning and selecting local ministers, how do we relate the idea of individual calling and the needs of the Church at that moment, with 'the people's choice' and the vicar's sense of 'rightness' about team composition? How do the bishop and diocese as a whole work in partnership with the local church on such compromises and definitions?

7 How important is the concept of permanence in matters of ministry? Traditionally it is linked firmly with ordination, but in practice it might be linked as much to stipendiary status and housing or to length of initial training. Are we giving enough energy to thinking this issue of permanence? What is the position of a member of a ministry team of several years' standing in comparison, say, with a paid youth worker, evangelist, pastoral assistant, Reader or ordained local minister? Where do matters of individual and team relate to this? We should resist the request to 'add' to traditional ministries those, say, of evangelist, pastoral assistant or eucharistic minister, so perpetuating a sense of a hierarchy of descending importance. The New Testament's understanding that *paradosis* is a task of the whole gospel community points more towards partnerships or teams, with

no standard pattern, of all whose different but equal ministries build up the people of God.

8 Should a diocesan policy on local ordination always emphasize that local ordained ministers should arise from within an existing ministry team rather than result from a sense of individual calling? Can the diocese cope with flexibility about this? Have we thought enough yet about the relation between non-stipendiary ministry and ordained local ministry?

9 It is increasingly clear that the stipendiary priesthood can no longer maintain the traditional functions of ministry as was probably the case 100 years ago. Are we clear that the Church of England, with or without ecumenical engagement, should still accept the responsibility of pastoral ministry to the whole population, which was the under-lying basis of that tradition? If so, should it not be affirmed clearly as the preamble to any coherent diocesan strategy for mission and ministry?

10 If a diocesan pattern becomes general and accepted, what is the bishop's place, especially about the conditions for and the practice of commissioning?

A third significant test for the development of diocesan Local Ministry lies in the critical dialogue between faith and the life of society. Christian practice and hope has its own proper *logos* or internal reasoning, founded on the saving events of the Christian story. Yet it also cannot be kept separate from ordinary life because it has a direct bearing on the struggle for truth of the whole of humanity, including the Church itself, and the entire creation. A local church cannot help looking at its context through the eyes of the human Jesus, the risen Christ, the distributing work of the Spirit, and the entire interweaving life of God in all creation. Is the Church to which we now aspire a true echo of God's life of genuine community and does it urgently but without anxiety press for those forms of life which we know to be a sign and foretaste of God's salvation for all?

CHAPTER 5

Preaching at Ordinations Now

I believe that none of us can cope with everything being held up for radical questioning all at the same time. So, for example, we find that those who are iconoclastic when it comes to biblical exegesis can be conservative in their approach to liturgical innovation. In a recent debate on continuing ministerial education, the anxiety was expressed that so far as ministerial thinking goes now, 'All cats are grey.' The debate will continue on whether baptized membership releases in the Church a rainbow of ministries, differing from one locality to another, reflecting the lack of blueprint in the New Testament churches, or whether ordained ministry, succeeding to the apostles, carries a great responsibility for the Church's mission and disperses lesser authorities to others.

One thing is clear to those who from time to time are called upon to preach at services of ordination for deacons and priests or the commissioning of Readers and ministry teams of various kinds: the present situation presents a dilemma. I find I cannot speak comfortably and reassuringly as though we were not in the eye of the storm on these matters. Equally, I can see the hard choices, the disciplined study, financial sacrifices, and constraints on families that are represented in the line of those to be ordained or commissioned. How can I say something of God's word now in the situation in which the Church is far from clear about what it means by this liturgical act, expressed in this set of words and liturgical expression we call the Ordinal? How can I at the same time – indeed how can the whole act of worship – both affirm all God's people in their work for the kingdom of so many kinds, and give proper congratulations, support, encouragement, warning and hope to candidates for particular ministries, lay and ordained?

Many today are asking radical questions about the role of Readers – are they really 'laity' or should some be recognized as 'ordained'? Others have strong conviction that it's a nonsense to call a transitional, probationary year of ordination leading to priesthood, 'the diaconate'. Why do we expect someone called to be a priest not to be 'made a priest' without becoming a deacon first (see Hallenbeck, 1996)? There is a gathering opinion that we should restore the diaconate as a full and equal part of the Church's threefold order, alongside the presbyterate and episcopate. Certainly the current ecumenical discussion on the nature of the Church and its ministry, the ecumenical commitments to further thought that have been entered into, and new understandings of the traditions and practices of the earliest Church require Anglicans to engage deeply with the question, 'What do we mean now by the diaconate in the Church?'

Then we have to return to questions such as, 'Why have some done so much training to be a Reader or deacon when others on Local Ministry teams or as pastoral assistants are given an apparently similar ministerial responsibility?' Some would ask whether the term 'ordination' the best one for making distinctions, especially in the light of what some would call the basic 'ordination' into ministry for the sake of the Kingdom of God which baptism bestows. What language would best help us to describe the distinctive yet united patterns of ministry that in a variety of contexts will pragmatically overlap (for example, the role of a Reader where there is no deacon or the role of a eucharistic minister where there is no Reader)? These issues will not be resolved in the short term but, meanwhile, ordination sermons are demanded of us for the whole range of category of ordinand – stipendiary or voluntary deacon or priest, and those who may move between these categories; ministers in secular employment, and members of Local Ministry teams who have also been called to ordination as deacons or priests.

The following two sermons in this chapter – one for deacons and one for priests – are in no way offered as models. Rather I include them here as a marker in a long process of trying to articulate liturgically – to candidates, families, friends, parishioners, ambivalent as well as supportive work colleagues and neighbour contacts – that in ordination we experience the paradox of something that has an absolute priority on our concern and resources and equally that is only one of the significant ways in which human beings can be called in the Church to serve God's coming Kingdom.

A sermon preached at the ordination of deacons in Gloucester Cathedral, June 2000

Is there a place any longer in Britain for God, Christ and the Church? And if not, is there really a place for Christianity? Those to be ordained deacon today will have pondered such questions long before now. Not least because from today you will be on the front line in a society where the privileged status of the Christian story is no longer accepted.

One of the New Testament words for describing the task of Churches literally means to 'hand over'. In the pages of the Bible that expression presents both a sinister and a positive picture. It's used of Jesus being handed over to the soldiers by Judas; of Pilate in turn handing over Jesus to the crowd; both Paul and Peter experienced being 'handed over' to the Roman authorities. Those of you who have been preparing for ordination and stood beside those who were may feel you already know something about being 'handed over' – will there be anything left, you may ask, of time, commitment, love, energy? But the New Testament also contains a very positive sense of 'handing over', meaning to preach the Good News of Jesus Christ. Paul writes:

> Now I should remind you, brothers and sisters, of the good news that I proclaimed to you, which you in turn received, in which also you stand, through which also you are being saved, if you hold firmly to the message that I proclaimed to you ... For I handed on to you as of first importance what I in turn had received.
>
> (1 Cor. 15.1–3)

He indicates a line of 'handing on' the tradition with authority, one witness taking over from another. He also speaks of the beginnings of the Eucharist in a similar way:

> For I received from the Lord what I also 'handed on' to you, that the Lord Jesus on the night when he was betrayed ('handed – over') took the loaf and when he had given thanks, he broke it.
>
> (1 Cor. 11.23–4)

So the two uses of 'handing on' come together in one sentence about the Eucharist. Bearing witness to the Christ as both a receiving and a handing on of the tradition is linked to our remembering that other 'handing over' which was Christ's betrayal.

In the Church today we talk a great deal about being a sign of God's mission. To be in the community of faith as one of the baptized is by definition to be part of the receiving and 'handing over' of the Good News of Christ. A generous appraisal of our efforts is that we are 'handing over' Christ in terms of both witness and betrayal every day of the week.

God takes a huge risk with us as Christ is delivered up for crucifixion again and again. But in this we learn that God is best known in vulnerability and daring. We make what we will of God's word and do what we will with the Church – because God has freely chosen to 'hand over' love with open hands.

A renewed sense of Church involves all the baptized in many ways of witnessing. But are we clear what we mean by mission now? In a multi-faith, multicultural, postmodern world how will a Christian community go about its witnessing? And where are deacons in the midst of all this?

We've grown up with the idea that being a deacon is mostly about menial service. But scholars have recently been giving us some fresh ideas. Ignatius, a bishop in the early Church, reminds us to 'show the deacons respect. They represent Christ.' This idea of representing a higher authority is a key. The etymology of *diakonia* at one time was linked with raising dust through hasty movement (Collins, 1990, p. 89). Although this is now pronounced naive, the picture of a fast-moving messenger in a dry climate raising the dust through running or driving a chariot has a powerfully evocative appeal for some (Maybee, 1998). How graphically this ties with the idea of deacon as a courier or go-between, a messenger urgently carrying important news from one person to another. Deacons are certainly those given commissioned authority to take a message. In church usage that has meant either authority from the bishop or from a Church. Recent research shows that the Church's earliest tradition on deacons includes the themes of being courier or spokesperson, agent or ambassador, and attendant on someone or a household to fulfil various tasks (see Collins, 1990). As Jesus served the Father, as a ransom for many (Mark 10.45), deacons have a mandate from God and from the Church to all people in need and a message back from the world to the Church. They literally have one foot in the sanctuary and one foot in the world. So they can be a bridge bringing messages from one to the other. We know that all congregations, all ministers at work, Local Ministry teams of many kinds, share Christ's mandate to preach the gospel at whatever cost – in one sense the New Testament shows that this is all the work of *diakonia*. The particular work of the deacon is precisely to remind us that everyone has a mandate to share the good news and to facilitate us in carrying it out rather than doing it while we watch. So, those ordained deacon are to model, lead, and encourage all the baptized in 'running through the dust' to hand over the gospel.

We've got two very powerful visual pictures here – the running to 'hand over' the message – so important it requires speed, effort, being out of breath, being fit, a minimum of baggage, knowing which way to go, pacing ourselves so that we can run the whole distance, expecting the satisfaction of reaching our destination – despite the pain – and perhaps most importantly still being able to remember the content of the message when, gasping, we arrive.

The other physical picture is of running through *dust*. Imagine the runner not only *covered* in dust but also having it the eyes, the hair, the mouth and lungs. As I was reflecting on this I happened to see a TV documentary on our complex relationship with dust. The programme invited us to become dust-friendly – to embrace bacteria, not run away from them. Recent research suggests that our immune system needs bacteria to work on – or else they start on healthy organs.

In our society dust is usually frowned upon – we pay good money to have it removed by machines or people. But running in dust and throwing it in the air is fun for children, and it looks spectacular when vehicles throw up dust clouds on a country road. I appreciate dust most when the sun catches it mid-air and suddenly there is a spectrum of colours offering a new light or perspective on God's world. It may be too fanciful to expect a messenger to appreciate the beauty of dust. But Isaiah says, 'How beautiful upon the mountains are the feet of the messenger . . . who brings good news' (52.7). What we all know is that goodness and beauty and loving service don't come without hard work and are often only glimpsed through the mess and dirt of everyday living.

But I've seen people dying of emphysema. Some have contracted very serious illness from the wrong kind of dust in their place of employment; many would say that their daily pressures could be likened to running through dust; so the ordained dust runner will have lots of connections with those at the wrong end of dust and could make common cause with those who need support in having their working or living environment made safer. There will be many times when preparing a sermon, wrestling with the best way to offer pastoral care or to resolve a conflict when we just have to live with the dust, hoping to see God's will somehow refracted in the half-light.

Whether at work, or in the ministry team or generally in a parish, the deacon is uniquely placed to assist the mission of everyone. The deacon can draw people together to work out what mission means in their circumstances, what language today best conveys the gospel message, how we speak of God to those whose life is in fragments, what kind of community life Christians should be fostering, what kind of encounter we should be having with people of other faith traditions, how we show that God is concerned not just for us but for the salvation of all creation. The deacon can also take a lead in encouraging, recruiting, training and organizing Christians to show Christ in loving service.

There are many churches today where it's just normal for there to be groups of laity supporting the bereaved or single-parent families, or taking school assemblies or preparing people for the sacraments. Here the deacon can help to locate training resources and enable laity to be more confident in their ministries.

A traditional note to understanding the ministry of the deacon is to think of following Christ in serving rather than dominating. Deacons have a special place in reminding all of us that wherever we serve God – in bank, shop, family, neighbourhood, on the motorway or in the parish and diocese – we do so in humility. Christians sometimes muddle up humility with lack of assertiveness or full use of our given role. Deacons could reflect on that and help us all to get clearer. Taking our proper part with pride is very important for the effective running of businesses, organizations, churches and families, but not at the expense of another.

As you adjust to this new representative role at work or in the parish you will receive support and encouragement from many sides: family, congregation, other clergy and public ministers, diocesan training, friends and colleagues at work. Above all, as deacons you remind everyone that our mission must reflect what we know of God's own character. Remember that doesn't have to be all talk – many of the prophets gave their message through symbols; Jesus showed the trans-forming power of God in having meals with groups of people of all kinds; Francis said, 'Preach the gospel, use words if you really must.'

Serving at table and meeting their need is another important image. The idea of serving and waiting at table – so characteristic of Jesus' ministry – is a profound thread in the Christian tradition. In a subtle and creative manner, Luke's account of the Last Supper adds richness to our under-standing of deaconing. Luke portrays God as a master who, returning tired from a journey, reverses role with his slaves and serves them at table. Here is a leader who is meeting the real needs of hungry people with humility. Jesus' God is one who aches for a world of mutuality and face-to-face meeting – for people with God, people with each other and with creation itself. God takes the risk of setting in the midst a few of us – bishops, priests and deacons – to keep us all in mind of what we are to be and do. This means partly just getting on with the ministry that opens before us as we recognize human need; but in the Church today it must be also about helping *the whole Church* to learn how to serve, how to be a go-between, how to see God's word through the dust.

We celebrate that a new path opens for you who are now to be made deacon. May you grow in your sense of being called both by your Church and personally by God; together with others may you deepen in your sense of being blessed by God and of being a source of blessing. When you worry that you make mistakes or lack conviction remember that in all of us there is an inextricable mixture of *handing over*. Jesus tells us we have no choice but to let wheat and tares grow together until the harvest – we cannot always tell at the time whether any particular act of *handing over* Christ will turn out to be witness or denial. Your chief calling, therefore, as you get dust in your ears and teeth through many ways of serving, is to grow daily in the love of God.

A sermon preached at the ordination of priests in Gloucester Cathedral, June 2000

From many churches and places we're here to surround with love those to be ordained priest today. It's an occasion for pride and celebration.

Each of us knows what the journey has been so far; we can only guess at what may be needed in the journey ahead. But we also know we cannot keep ordination in a place by itself. We've discovered too much about God's call for all Christian people to work together in partnership to put priests on a pedestal.

Let's try to put ordination in perspective without for a moment denying the importance and wonder of today. On 16 April 1963 a young clergyman sat in the Birmingham, Alabama, city jail. His crime was to have led a civil-rights march. Sitting in his cell that day Martin Luther King Jnr wrote a letter asking searching questions about the character of a Church. An especially telling paragraph includes these passionate words:

> I have travelled the length and breadth of Alabama, Mississippi and the Southern States. On sweltering summer days and crisp autumn mornings. I have looked at her beautiful Churches with their spires pointing heavenward. Over and over again I have found myself asking, Who worships here? Who is their God?
>
> (Jinkins, 1999, p. 85)

So who is our God? What do we believe is God's passionate desire for us and all creation – what Jesus called the Kingdom of God? What kind of Church would we have to be to serve that desire? Each of us will have different answers from our own experiences of God's love and ways of being a human being and being formed by various Churches. In a bewildered world surely our urgent task as a Church is to gather the fragments and listen to those whom the powerful regularly exclude. A Church that serves God's mission will be working with others to bring wholeness in relationship between persons, in local communities and in the wider fields of nation and world.

Across the world, Churches are recalling that they know quite a lot about relating because the God we name and worship as Father, Son and Spirit is a community of three different persons inviting relationship. All the baptized members of the Church might think of ourselves as an ever-deepening spiral of meeting with God in the everyday stuff of working and living. We could imagine a world reflecting our trinitarian God stepped to the contagious rhythm of a round dance, calypso or reggae where dancers are free yet held together in the music. Scientists are finding the same dynamic God in the double helix, the continuing and connected movement of oceans, volcanoes and landmasses, the many successive but always unique coming of seasons, and the fragile inter-action between apparently separate forms of animal life.

Jesus came to show us God's exuberant energy and abundance – water into wine, lepers cleansed, debts forgiven, outcasts pulled in, religious laws ridiculed, and the dead raised. Jesus creates face-to-face community, where everyone counts; women, children and men have equal place, the last comes first, and there is a genuine intention to act out 'Your Kingdom come on earth as in heaven' – for the sick, the prisoner, the naked, and the hungry. 'How are you showing your responsibility for the least of these?' asks Jesus' God to Churches everywhere.

Our overwhelmingly generous God invites us to obedience whether our ministry is in the everyday world or parish – Do this in remembrance of me; eat and drink bread and wine until I come again; wash one another's feet as a way of life.

Those being ordained today will all have different focuses to your work – and over the years these will vary. One of the chief ways we think of priests is as those who lead worship and especially the Holy Communion, the Eucharist. Many of us think of the Eucharist as the heartbeat of the Church; a condensation of all that Christianity means, a dress rehearsal for the life in all its fullness which is Jesus' promise and gift. When we come together to celebrate the Eucharist it will always be a different situation but it will always inform and expand our understanding of God, mission, Church and therefore priesthood. I owe a debt of gratitude to David Ford who in his recent book, *Self and Salvation*, has pointed out four particular elements in this process on which I should like now briefly to reflect.

In Holy Communion, first, we are blessed and learn to become a source of blessing to others. We come face to face with Jesus, receive God's abundant life and learn to reach out to others and all creation. Second, we are placed. Estate agents say location is the key to house-buying. For Churches, location is the key to mission – our involvement and concern for a particular spot; in the Eucharist we are placed before Christ's face, the faces of all other disciples and faces of all who need us – and our own faces are transfigured from glory to glory.

Third, in Holy Communion we are timed. The Eucharist links past, present and future; it links us with Christ, Paul and Francis, Benedict and Wesley; it puts our overfilled diaries into heavenly perspective; it links us today with the hour of our dying. Finally, in the Eucharist we are commanded: 'Do this in remembrance of me.' We voluntarily put ourselves under obedience to Christ, available for God's mission, to die to self, to see everything from God's angle.

If we had time we could produce a longer list of what is going on in Church and Eucharist but certainly these four elements are true for every church member. The added and vital work of the priest is so to preside in the mission, the life and the Eucharist of the Church – and for some, to show us all how to be an influence for Christ in daily work – that together we can grow in being Church for God's kingdom. Let's look at the list again: blessed, placed, timed, and commanded. The priest is one who assures us of God's blessing in all the differing callings we have – at work, in the neighbourhood, family and Church. She is saying to us, 'Yes, I see that is your ministry – what support will you need so that it can deepen and you can flourish in it? Equally the priest may sometimes be challenging and asking awkward questions about the way we go about our lives. The priest takes a special responsibility for the good ordering of the community life – checking out who feels included, excluded; what is the relationship between young and old, adult and child, men and women; for whom is this church certainly not a source of blessing and what might be done about it?

Second, in the Eucharist we are all placed. So we talk of the priest as the one who presides in the worship of that local church or cluster of churches, who knows to his fingertips the feel of the place, all the different communities of interest and conflict, the joys and pains, the hopes and fears and the Church's serving mission there. The priest will want to work with others using all the range of human insights to ensure the effective mission of the local church in parish, schools and places of work. Also he knows how to stand beside people when their need is great – and can also teach all of us to be witnesses when our moment comes. The priest is one who as a baptized member, but also as called to be in charge, can help everyone to know their true place and grow into it: the one who can help relate this church to all other churches and communities.

Third, the priest checks that we know we are timed. She will ensure that whatever time of life we are in, we have an equal place and voice; if we are in the heat of child-rearing or in the pressures of business, career or service to others, she will make time to help us see the connections with God's love and purpose. Spiritual guidance – call it what you like – will be a priority for all; if your life is in turmoil, she will make sure someone is there for you, just as much as when your time is up. She will remind us that we haven't got for ever – 'The time has come, repent and believe the gospel.' The eucharistic life is about living in the Christian tradition – always the same and always new, non-identical repetition – the jazz factor in God's life discovered through worship that is at once carefully prepared and adventurously performed.

Finally, knowing that we are commanded. The priest knows about sin, forgiveness and reconciliation. He knows his own places of brokenness as channels of grace; he doesn't just show us shiny success. The priest who most influenced me as a young man struggled with acute shell shock throughout his ministry. The priest will know how we can go on spelling out our mission in new times and places; will remind us not to be trees that give no fruit, nor to be those who bury our talents in the ground or who refuse to serve the poor; he will know how we can find education and training to open us more usefully into working with God; and most important of all – bearing in mind the Last Supper where Jesus gave us God's new commandment – how to celebrate, have fun and enjoy a good feast together.

All this may seem very ambitious, knowing clergy as we do. So often we seem a rough, broken, ragged, spiritually bankrupt bunch of women and men. No wonder they say the Church is going down the tubes. Well, isn't that the point – dying to live? It's only when we know our utter need for God that we're any good. Look at the beginnings of God's Church – look at the disciples; look at the bizarre bunch of people to whom Jesus gives new life; look at Jesus dying on the cross deserted by his friends; look at Jesus' broken body in Mary's arms; look at those who share the peace in your local church week by week.

Recall the questions of Martin Luther King Jnr: 'Who worships here? Who is their God?' God's nature is revealed in weakness, ambiguity and mystery. Just supposing the harassed, chaotic, disorganized, patronizing, out-of-touch and frequently divided Church shows the world how to live only from God's energy. Any words and actions of those we ordain priest today depend totally on God's life in them. Thankfully our belief has no other foundation.

Conclusion

I'm conscious that readers having got to here may be disappointed that I have offered no great synthesis or articulation of future models for the Church's ministry. So what has been achieved in the writing of yet another book about the Church? I see it as a contribution to the field of enquiry about 'What Church does God call for in this place and time?' We are situated in a medium-term – perhaps 100 years – reformation of Anglicanism. But it's not even as neat as that for within the larger scale are situated many smaller overlapping movements, like slurs over a music stave inviting the musician to play these bars together. It's also part of the character of Anglican Christianity that it's never 'sorted' because as Church we are *semper reformanda*. I have assumed that theories and decisions about the future of the Church for the sake of the common good or God's Kingdom will require the interdisciplinary co-operation of many fields of knowledge that may appear to be separated but in reality are not. Furthermore the Church's membership consists of thousands of people who both are expert in their fields and can see that true knowledge lies in their speaking to one another so that many partial truths may come together in a fuller wisdom.

Of course thinking about the nature and task of the Church is relatively unimportant if we continue to associate it mainly with the limited concerns of clergy and their chosen helpers to keep something going; Church is unimportant if we see it excluding all that we do when we're busy in our primary vocations of so many kinds. In support of traditional notions of hierarchy, I meet many, perhaps the majority of church members, who continue to believe in a Church not stepped to the contagious rhythm of the salsa or reggae, but rather to the laws of great and small, important and not important – the world of the effective new rector who 'lands running' and for whom the expression 'significant parish' has a definite meaning. I meet laity and clergy who believe that what God wants is for the majority to lead a relatively blameless life, conscientiously carrying out their daily business, showing compassion for the weak, caring for their family, supporting funds to pay for building repairs and clergy stipends and going to church regularly. This leaves the clergy, together with Readers and youth workers to be 'ministers', paid to represent God to the world in relevant words and unimpeachable behaviour. Those bishops and clergy whose picture of Church overlaps with much of this are often, in my experience, notably compassionate, pastorally alert and striving to hold back the pressures of overwork with a deep spirituality as well as wrestling with the hot issues of the day. Their preferred word for what most of the laity are called to is often 'discipleship', not 'ministry'.

This book, always assuming we are all working in a single field with many points of contact, has taken the radically opposed view, supported largely by some most persuasive strands of the contemporary, international, ecumenical, theological dialogue on these issues. I believe the Christian tradition from the earliest times – often in practice subverted by different generations of religious experts – is that to be a baptized member of the society inspired by the resurrection and Pentecost (of which Christian 'community' is a developed form) is by definition to be part of the ordering of Christ's sacramental presence and of the whole work of God dispersed in the world. At many times in the Church's relatively short life – in terms of the age of the planet, the unfolding history of humanity and of other world faiths – paid professional, set-aside clerics have been significant leaders. Many have led heroic lives and been instrumental in initiatives against social evils and injustice. This constantly variable pattern has produced both clericalism and anticlericalism. It has produced dependency as well as profound frustration in 'small' or 'on the edge' churches. The plaques on church walls bear testimony both to the warm admiration and affection in which many of the clerical profession have been held as well as how the history of churches has been episodic, oscillating with the varying goals and prohibitions of successive office holders.

In my overview of most Anglican churches now, I suggested we still largely believe in, as well as feel free to criticize and scapegoat, a clerical hierarchy – with a few keen lay helpers and supporters. This is not an accusation of immorality but a statement of fact; we collude at this together for very deep reasons. And also we are now standing at another of those countless points of liminality which the Church, along with all other major organizations and prevalent networks, must experience. We stand on the threshold of something new but cannot yet tell what or how it will be. We know the sources of pain – the waning of support for worship and for giving sufficient money to pay the bills for the inherited patterns of ministry, the irritating fact that churches that have abandoned a concern for a particular location are prospering in regional centres (even at our expense), the reality that many clergy are due to retire and that we have no way of replacing them, and the persistence of hierarchical patterns of church life which our theological roots cannot condone.

So what shall we do? We know of the galaxy of writing and talking about new ways of being a missionary congregation. We are invited to a relational ecclesiology rooted in those pictures of God, which though always imperfect, suggest more about interaction and mutuality than gradations of power. Many of us are experimenting daily with new forms of church life. The Holy Spirit seems now to be inviting us to be a Church:

- where everyone in the whole of life can make an equal but different response to the call to be part of Christ's united but kaleidoscopic ministry;
- that cuts ice with the poorest and the excluded and with those growing parts of ourselves that yearn for intimacy, demand honesty and need to walk with others;
- that stops playing at centuries past;
- that echoing Godself meets people at their point of pain and remains there;
- that shows the way in not treating the planet as the mere background for increasing our personal prosperity at the cost of another;
- that is shaped by God's regenerative power and restorative healing and that can help others to know what we already partially experience;
- that shows the world its true life by daring to choose to be at one with the risky, distributive and serving energy we call God's Spirit.

Unrenovated churches become bored, despairing, redundant for most people and must face death. This is not to be overdramatic or irresponsible. The Body of Christ knows resurrection only through death – and then not with prior certainty. 'The Church is, as we individually are, baptismally drenched in the death of Christ' (Jinkins, 1999, p. 30). History books show how whole legions of Christian Churches have fought each other for supremacy, vied with each other and closely related faiths for superior accreditation (Armstrong, 1999), and many have marched over the horizon into proper oblivion. Churches in other words should be well versed in dealing with death, even their own:

> The irony, of course, is that each Eucharist feast the Church celebrates ... calls it to do precisely this, to offer up in the Spirit of Christ and thereby to embrace its unique and irreplaceable identity in the world of which it is reminded in the sacraments. The Church meets death in the death of Christ at the Lord's Table. It consumes and is nourished by the continual self-offering of Christ. It feeds on Christ's body and blood. Yet the Church does not seem to anticipate its own consumption, its own offering, its sacrifice when it moves

from liturgy to political externality, from poetry to prose. But the Marcan text (8.31–38) does anticipate it: 'If any want to become my followers, let them deny themselves and take up their cross and follow me.'

(Jinkins, 1999, pp. 29f.)

Of course the Church is dying; that's its only way to know resurrection, going down the tubes into God's unfolding future. As Brueggemann reminds us, death includes mourning, not as an option but as 'the only door and route to joy', which God who mourns in ways unknown to us can teach to us (Brueggemann, 1978, pp.112f.). But we are called not to a spirit of hopelessness or even petulance that things have to change. Now is the time to rediscover our vocation by digging deep into our foundations and allowing for the reordering and renovation of the Church. If we take the view that it's only clergy basically who minister to the rest of us who get on with God's mission in the world, then the ordering of the Church doesn't matter all that much. However, if we believe that as the people of God together in equality and difference we have the capacity to become an ever-deepening spiral of engagement with the whole of God's life in the whole of God's world, that our high calling is to show the world its true life, then our mutual and external ordering, relating and orientations need to be constantly renovated signs of God's character, work and hope. All our ways of doing Church are an open book to be publicly read and so the words and pictures on the page need to represent life in all its fullness for all.

How shall we progress this concern to meet and address our unique vocation as Church, unconcerned with our particular institutional and denominational survival? We have become accustomed to the increasing rate of production of programmes, strategies and tools for improving our churches that spin out of bishops' studies and councils and synods, from training officers and the Internet. Provided they allow for dialogue, engagement and communal learning, we have need for practical wisdom of this kind. Leaders of church community – in diocese, school, parish, university, industry, hospital or prison – hold the particular task of ensuring there is adequate facilitation of holistic, systemic reflection and the provision of conditions in which church community can develop more fully. Unless some of us take responsibility for the creation of the necessary conditions for Church to happen, especially through the deepening of the prayerful thought of the whole Church we shall continue in the present spiral of energy loss.

Daniel W. Hardy reminds us that we have nothing to fear in the Church's present upheavals, as 'Disorder may be an essential stage of reordering' (Hardy, 1993, p. 5). Mary Grey, speaking of the postmodern

Church, suggests we require an approach that leans into the mystery of God (see Grey, 1997b, p. 9). David Bohm in his reflection on creativity which I discussed in Chapter 2, insists that when we have a cluster of problems together we do not solve them separately or mechanically, but in a spirit of contemplation, intuitively allowing the picture slowly to focus and bring us to new levels of understanding, 'a vast harmony of order of indescribable beauty' (Bohm, 1998, p. 11). He urges the use of our creative imagination to come to new order, structure, harmony and totality, which we are instinctively searching for but currently have not the vocabulary to define. Bohm reflects on the example of Anne Sullivan, teacher of Helen Keller who was blind and deaf from an early age. Keller experienced water in a wide variety of ways and only gradually through the complete love of her teacher, came to connect the totality of those experiences with the frequent marking out of the shape of the word 'water' in the palm of her hand. Disorder, insists Bohm, does not exist, but we need to learn new language, words and concepts so that new concepts and structures can connect with and stretch our experience of living in the world. In a similar way, although the rereading and debating accounts of the theological ideas of our forebears can be a great comfort, in the end this can be no substitute for pressing on to find the ones we need for today and tomorrow.

Bohm properly warns against the temptation of believing that the discovering of mechanical solutions will be a satisfactory substitute for the time-consuming emergence of creative and original patterns. This invitation to think through our imaginations should be written up over the doors of every provincial, diocesan and parish office for when the temptation arises to believe there can be fast, achievable solutions:

> People have been led to believe that anything and everything can be obtained if only one has the right techniques and methods. What is needed is to be aware of the ease with which the mind slips comfortably back into this age-old pattern. Certain kinds of things can be achieved by techniques and formulae, but originality and creativity are not among these. The act of seeing this deeply (and not merely verbally or intellectually) is also the act in which originality and creativity can be born.
>
> (Bohm, 1998, p. 26)

Each period of history produces its own language and concepts to explain its understanding of the world's ordering. Bohm encourages all of us, whatever our path or field of intelligence, to take our particular part in leaving behind safe and tried preconceptions. Instead we can choose to perceive the world in a fresh way, feeling out and exploring – in a way that has coherence with past work – new and creative ideas that will liberate everyone. This seems to be a significant invitation for all of us to pursue together as a combination of realism and hope.

In her invitation to allow the future to form itself through a mystical process, Grey seems not to be advocating an otherworldly, individualistic pietism. Her theology is usually in dialogue with those who have known God's apparent absence or who can no longer speak easily of God in the face of overwhelming suffering – Hillesum, Jantzen, Merton and Ruether, to name just a few. I warm to her quotation from Catherine Keller, 'We meet God as the molten core of heart's desire, energizing our courage and our quest' (Grey, 1997b, p. 27). As that part of human society describing ourselves as 'Church', in a spirit of steady stillness, like a flame flickering but not quenched, I believe we do need to rediscover a mystical approach for the rediscovery of identity. However estranged we may feel from our Church's structures and behaviour, we have the promise that the life we live together is Christ living within, inspiring, stretching and opening up in us new paths (cf. Gal. 2.20). The Gospel of John reminds us we are a trinitarian communion of those who live by Christ's blood, dwell in the vine, united in immense diversity, bearing rich fruit. The love and energy we produce in mutual relation is ordered by the same Spirit that shapes the stars and solar systems. We shall find the ways to relate to each other and to the whole creation precisely in our relating to God who comes to meet us often in ways beyond our immediate understanding but also invites us to join with him in passionate imagining and searching for the salvation of all things. The God who meets us in intimacy as well as the dark night, says to us as to Isaiah, 'The Spirit of the Lord GOD is upon me, because the LORD has anointed me; he has sent me to bring good news to the oppressed, to bind up the broken-hearted, to proclaim liberty to the captives, and release to the prisoners' (Isa. 61.1).

In coherence with the past, we are called to be a sign of God with us, and therefore a sign of deep compassion as well as a non-anxious presence, like Jesus in the boat on the lake in the storm, or an experienced midwife with a family facing a difficult birth, or a seasoned mountain rescue team with frightened people who have gone beyond their limits. There comes a time when explanations and frantic procedures must be gently overtaken by touch, silence and calm. The outcome is not yet known, but a still, patient, holistic trust dispels a spirit of fear or blame, holding everyone in a web of hope.

Of course the Church as we know it is gradually collapsing – it cannot survive in its old forms much longer. We need to know and receive God's compassion for us in our flailing around, trying to put off the day when our once proud body becomes a corpse. Using all our points of wisdom – about God's nature, God's hope for all creation, God's task for the

Church and our mutual parts within that – we can reach out for what is coming next. It is already partly visible, in Jesus Christ, taking the form of a slave and humbled on the cross and in the ecumenical field of international church and world life today in the work of the Spirit. However, in the context of recognizing the maturity of living without certainty in a world of unresolved restless potential, maybe we can be content without an elegant, predictable church. Let us find new energy in a humble, questioning company of belief with blurred and jagged edges. The mystical tradition of silence, of taking nothing for the journey, and of singing, 'nothing, nothing, nothing', can bring a frightening sense of absence. But those who have led the practice and invited others to share it, witness to the reality of being carried into new stages and glimpsing a new world. The contemporary mystical theologian and retreat guide, William Johnston, expresses it in this way:

> Whereas the chief characteristic of infused contemplation is the sense of presence, the mystical state is preceded by a painful sense of absence. Indeed, it is preceded by a harrowing experience that can bring the mystic to the brink of despair and to nervous collapse. But the dark night does not last forever. Time comes when the log of wood, hitherto damp and sodden, catches fire and begins to burn brightly. The winter is past. The rain is over and gone. 'Arise, my love, my dove, my beautiful one and come away', Song of Songs 2.10.
>
> (Johnston, 2000, p. 102)

In seeking to respond now to God with originality about the Church, we don't have to force our creativity, but to let it come to be through us – in company with every other person in the field – and perhaps slowly find words, stories, pictures, sounds and symbols to express what we are coming to know. Jesus invites 'anyone with ears to hear' (Mark 4.9). If we each play our part from where we stand in letting the energy flow, not least through our quiet waiting on God, we shall receive 'thirty, sixty and a hundredfold'.

Bibliography

Abrashoff, D. Michael, 2001. 'Retention through Redemption', *Harvard Business Review*, February, pp. 137ff.

Anderson, Ray S., 1999. 'Living in the Spirit', in Ray S. Anderson (ed.), *Theological Foundations for Ministry: Selected Readings for a Theology of Church in Ministry*, Edinburgh, T. & T. Clark.

Antone, Hope S., 2000. 'AWRC: Daring to Dream', *Ministerial Formation*, Geneva, WCC, 88, pp. 47ff.

Arbogast, Marianne, 1994. 'Liberating the Baptized: Shared Ministry in Northern Michigan', *The Witness*, 1249 Washington Rd, Suite 3115, Detroit, Michigan, August/September, pp. 8ff.

ARCIC Anglican–Roman Catholic International Commission, 1982. *Final Report*, London, CTS/SPCK.

Armstrong, Karen, 1999. *A History of God*, London, Vintage.

Armstrong, Regis J., 1994. *St Francis of Assisi: Writings for a Gospel Life*, London, St Paul's.

Avis, Paul, 2000. *The Anglican Understanding of the Church: An Introduction*, London, SPCK.

Bacon, Hannah and Jobling, J'annine, 2000. 'Why Feminists Should still be Liberals', in J. Jobling and I. Markham (eds), pp. 91ff.

Barnett, James Monroe, 1995. *The Diaconate: A Full and Equal Order*, Pennsylvania, Trinity Press International, revised edition.

Baum, Gregory (ed.), 1999. *The Twentieth Century: A Theological Overview*, Maryknoll, New York, Orbis.

Bishops' Conference of England and Wales, 1995. *The Sign We Give*, Chelmsford, Matthew James.

Boff, Leonardo, 1985. *Saint Francis: A Model for Human Liberation*, London, SCM.

Boff, Leonardo, 1986. *Ecclesiogenesis: The Base Communities Reinvent the Church*, London, Collins.

Boff, Leonardo, 1992. *Trinity and Society*, London, Burns & Oates.

Bohm, David, 1995. *Wholeness and the Implicate Order*, London and New York, Routledge.

Bohm, David, 1998, in L. Nichol (ed.), *On Creativity*, London and New York, Routledge.

Borgeson, Josephine and Wilson, Lynne (eds), 1990. *Reshaping Ministry: Essays in Memory of Wesley Frensdorff*, Diocese of Michigan.

Borgmann, Albert, 1992. *Crossing the Postmodern Divide*, Chicago and London, University of Chicago Press.

Bowden, Andrew and West, Michael, 2000. *Dynamic Local Ministry*, London, Continuum.

Brierley, Peter, 2000. *The Tide is Running Out: What the English Church Attendance Survey Tells Us*, London, Christian Research.

British Council of Churches, 1989. *The Forgotten Trinity 1: The Report of the BCC Study Commission of Trinitarian Doctrine Today*, London, BCC.

Brueggemann, Walter, 1978. *The Prophetic Imagination*, Philadelphia, Fortress Press.

Cavanaugh, William T., 1998. *Torture and Eucharist: Theology, Politics, and the Body of Christ*, Oxford, Blackwell.

Church House Publishing, 1997. *Shaping Ministry for a Missionary Church: A Review of Diocesan Ministry Strategy Documents*, London, CHP.

Church House Publishing, 2001. *Mind the Gap: Integrated Continuing Ministerial Education for the Church's Ministers*, London, CHP.

Church Times, 2000. Pat Ashworth, Reform Rejects Bid for 400 'C' Parishes, p. 4, 13 October.

Clark, Stephen, 2000, in R. Page, 2000.

Collins, John N., 1990. *Diakonia: Re-interpreting the Ancient Sources*, Oxford, Oxford University Press.

D'Costa, Gavin, 2000. *The Meeting of Religions and the Trinity*, Edinburgh, T. & T. Clark.

De Lubac, H., 1949. *Catholicism*, London, Burns, Oates & Washbourne.

Diocese of Birmingham, 1999. *Shaping Ministry*, Birmingham, Diocese of Birmingham.

Diocese of Chelmsford, 2000. *Bishop's Working Group on Ordained Local Ministry*, Chelmsford, Diocese of Chelmsford, May.

Diocese of Derby, 1998. *A Better Way: Diocesan Strategy for Ministry*, Derby, Diocese of Derby.

Diocese of Newcastle, 1992. *Hunter Valley Research Foundation Report*, Diocese of Newcastle, Newcastle, Australia.

Diocese of Newcastle, 1996. *Report of Ministry Review Committee*, Diocese of Newcastle, Newcastle, Australia.

Doctorow, E. L., 2000. *City of God*, London, Little, Brown & Co.

Doctrine Commission of the Church of England, 1995. *The Mystery of Salvation: A Report to General Synod*, CHP.

Douglas, Mary, 1994. *Risk and Blame: Essays in Cultural Theory*, London and New York, Routledge.

Dunn, D. G., 1992. *Jesus' Call to Discipleship*, Cambridge, Cambridge University Press.

Dyson, Freeman J., 1999. *The Sun, The Genome, and the Internet: Tools of Scientific Revolutions*, New York, New York Public Library; Oxford, Oxford University Press.

Elizondo, Virgilio, 1999. 'Emergence of a World Church and the Irruption of the Poor', in G. Baum (ed.), 1999.

Evans, G. R. and Percy, Martyn, 2000. *Managing the Church: Order and Organisation in a Secular Age*, Sheffield, Sheffield Academic Press.

Fenhagen, James C., with Hahn, Celia, 1995. *Ministry for New Times: Case Study for Change*, New York, Alban Institute.

Fergusson, David, and Sarot, Marcel, 2000. *The Future as God's Gift: Explorations in Christian Eschatology*, Edinburgh, T. & T. Clark.

Ford, David F., 1999. *Self and Salvation: Being Transformed*, Cambridge, Cambridge University Press.

Ford, David F. and Stamps, Dennis L., 1996. *Essentials of Christian Community: Essays for Daniel W. Hardy*, Edinburgh, T. & T. Clark.

Forrester, Duncan B., 2000. *Truthful Action: Explorations in Practical Theology*, Edinburgh, T. & T. Clark.

Forrester, Duncan B., 2001, *On Human Worth*, London, SCM.

Fullan, M., 1993. *Change Forces: Probing the Depths of Educational Reform*, London, The Falmer Press.

Gerloff, Roswith, 2000. 'An African Continuum in Variation: The African Christian Diaspora in Britain', *Black Theology: A Journal of Contextual Praxis*, 4.

Getui, Mary, 1999. 'Africa, Church and Theology: Do They Need Each Other?', *Ministerial Formation*, WCC, January.

Girard, René, 1987. *Things Hidden since the Foundation of the World*, London, Athlone.

Grant, George P., 1999, in G. Baum (ed.), 1999.

Greenwood, Robin, 1996. *Practising Community: The Task of the Local Church*, London, SPCK.

Greenwood, Robin, 2000a. *The Ministry Team Handbook: Local Ministry as Partnership*, London, SPCK.

Greenwood, Robin, 2000b. *Transforming Priesthood: A New Theology of Mission and Ministry*, London, SPCK.

Grey, Mary C., 1997a. *Beyond the Dark Night: A Way Forward for the Church?* London, Cassell.

Grey, Mary C., 1997b. *Prophecy and Mysticism: The Heart of the Postmodern Church*, Edinburgh, T. & T. Clark.

Grey, Mary C., 1999. 'Disturbing the Wise? Or the Wisdom of the Disturbed? Liberating Truth and Theological Education', in S. C. Barton (ed.), *Where Shall Wisdom be Found? Wisdom in the Bible, the Church and the Contemporary World*, Edinburgh, T. & T. Clark.

Grey, Mary C., 2000a. 'Exploring a Contemporary Doctrine of God with Special Reference to God the Father', *The British Journal of Theological Education*, 11 January, pp. 57ff.

Grey, Mary C., 2000b. *The Outrageous Pursuit of Hope: Prophetic Dreams for the Twenty-first Century*, London, Darton, Longman & Todd.

Gribbin, John, 1984. *In Search of Schrodinger's Cat: Quantum Physics and Reality*, London, Black Swan.

Gunton, Colin, 1998. *The Triune Creator: A Historical and Systematic Survey*, Edinburgh, Edinburgh University Press.

Hallenbeck, Edwin F. (ed.), 1996. *The Orders of Ministry: Reflections on Direct Ordination*, North American Association for the Diaconate, Providence, Rhode Island.

Hastings, Adrian, 1986. *A History of English Christianity*, London, Collins.

Hardy, Daniel W., 1993, in H. Regan and A.J. Torrance (eds), *Christ and Context*, Edinburgh, T. & T. Clark.

Hardy, Daniel W., 1996. *God's Ways with the World: Thinking and Practising Christian Faith*, Edinburgh, T. & T. Clark.

Hawkins, Thomas R., 1997. *The Learning Congregation: A New Vision of Leadership*, Louisville, Kentucky, Westminster John Knox Press.

Healy, Nicholas M., 2000. *Church, World and the Christian Life: Practical-Prophetic Ecclesiology*, Cambridge, Cambridge University Press.

Hendry, Joy, 1999. *An Introduction to Social Anthropology: Other People's Worlds*, London, Macmillan.

Hiley, B. J. and Peat, F. David (eds), 1988. *Quantum Implications: Essays in Memory of David Bohm*, London, Routledge.

Holloway, Richard, 1999. *Godless Morality: Keeping Religion out of Ethics*, Edinburgh, Canongate.

House of Bishops, 1997. *Eucharistic Presidency: A Theological Statement by the House of Bishops*, London, Church House Publishing.

House of Bishops, 2001. *The Eucharist: Sacrament of Unity: An Occasional Paper of the House of Bishops of the Church of England*, London, Church House Publishing.

Hull, John M., 1991. *What Prevents Christian Adults from Learning?* Philadelphia, Trinity Press International.

Jaworski, Joseph, 1998. *Synchronicity: The Inner Path of Leadership*, San Francisco, Barrett-Koehler.

Jenkins, Timothy, 1999a. *Religion in English Everyday Life: An Ethnographical Approach*, New York, Oxford, Berghahn Books.

Jenkins, Timothy, 1999b. 'Taking Local Seriously', *Ministry*, vol. 2, edn 4.

Jinkins, David, 1999. *The Church Faces Death: Ecclesiology in a Post-Modern Context*, Oxford, Oxford University Press.

Jobling, J'annine and Markham, Ian (eds), 2000. *Theological Liberalism: Creative and Critical*, London, SPCK.

Johns, Cheryl Bridges, 1999. 'The Meaning of Pentecost for Theological Education', *Ministerial Formation*, Geneva, WCC, 87, pp. 42ff.

Johnson, Elizabeth A., 1998. *She Who Is: The Mystery of God in Feminist Theological Discourse*, New York, Crossroad Herder.

Johnston, William, 2000. *'Arise my Love ...' Mysticism for a New Era*, Maryknoll, New York, Orbis.

King, Peter, 1995. *Dark Night Spirituality: Contemplation and the New Paradigm*, London, SPCK.

Küng, Hans, 1968. *The Church*, London, Search Press.

LaCugna, Catherine Mowry, 1991. *God for Us: The Trinity and Christian Life*, New York, HarperCollins.

Lakeland, Paul, 1997. *Postmodernity: Christian Identity in a Fragmented Age*, Minneapolis, Fortress Press.

Lampe, G. W. H., 1949. *Some Aspects of the New Testament Ministry*, London, SPCK.

Latner, Joel, 1983. 'This is the Speed of Light: Field and Systems Theories in Gestalt Theory', *Gestalt Journal*, vol. VI, no. 2, pp. 71ff.

Layzer, David, 1990. *Cosmogenesis: The Growth of Order in the Universe*, Oxford, Oxford University Press.

Le Carré, John, 2000. *A Small Town in Germany*, London, Hodder & Stoughton.

Legood, Giles, 2000. 'Liberal Theology and Church Structures', in J. Jobling and I. Markham (eds), 2000, pp. 126ff.

Loughlin, Gerard, 1997, 'René Girard (born 1923): Introduction', in Graham Ward (ed.), *The Postmodern God: A Theological Reader*, Oxford, Blackwell.

Marshall, Ian and Zohar, Danielah, 1997. *Who's Afraid of Schrodinger's Cat? The New Science Revealed: Quantum Theory, Relativity, Chaos and the New Cosmology*, London, Bloomsbury.

Maybee, Maylanne, 1998. 'Servanthood Through the Dust: Why the Diaconate?' in *Ministry Matters*, vol. 5, no. 3, pp. 6ff.

McKenna, Megan, 1994. *Not Counting Women and Children: Neglected Stories from the Bible*, Maryknoll, New York, Orbis.

McPartlan, Paul, 1993. *The Eucharist Makes the Church: Henri de Lubac and John Zizioulas in Dialogue*, Edinburgh, T. & T. Clark.

McPartlan, Paul, 1995. *Sacrament of Salvation: An Introduction to Eucharistic Ecclesiology*, Edinburgh, T. & T. Clark.

Metz, Johann Baptist, 1980. *Faith in History and Society: Toward a Practical Fundamental Theology*, London, Burns & Oates.

Moltmann, Jürgen, 1967. *Theology of Hope: On the Ground and the Implications of a Christian Eschatology*, London, SCM.

Moltmann, Jürgen, 1977. *The Church in the Power of the Spirit*, London, SCM.

Moltmann, Jürgen, 1989a. *Creating a Just Future: The Politics and Ethics of Creation in a Threatened World*, London, SCM.

Moltmann, Jürgen, 1989b. *The Trinity and the Kingdom of God: The Doctrine of God*, London, SCM.

Morisy, Ann, 1997. *Beyond the Good Samaritan: Community, Ministry and Mission*, London, Mowbray.

Mtetemala, Donald, 1999. 'Crossing the River into the Third Millennium: Address of Archbishop Donald Mtetemala to the 11th Synod of the Anglican Church of Tanzania', *The Anitepam Bulletin*, Washington, no. 24, November, pp. 14ff.

Müller-Fahrenholz, Geiko, 2000. *The Kingdom and the Power: The Theology of Jürgen Moltmann*, London, SCM.

Nathan, Ronald A., 2000. 'Pan-Africanism: What of the Twenty-First Century? A British Program', *Black Theology in Britain: A Journal of Contextual Praxis*, Sheffield Academic Press, issue 4, pp. 9–21.

Neale, Chohan, 2001. 'Family Constellations: Practical Considerations: Interview with Hunter Beaumont', *Systemic Solutions Bulletin*, pp. 4ff.

Njoroge, Nyambura J., 1998. 'Turn to God Rejoice in Hope', *Ministerial Formation*, Geneva, WCC, 83, October, pp. 4ff.

O'Murchu, Diarmuid, 1997. *Quantum Theology: Spiritual Implications of the New Physics*, New York, Crossroad.

Padfield, Deborah (ed.), 1999. *Hidden Lives: Stories from the East End by the People of 42 Balaam Street*, Newham, Eastside Community Heritage.

Page, Ruth, 2000. *God with Us: Synergy in the Church*, London, SCM.

Palmer, Parker, 1998. *The Courage to Teach: Exploring the Inner Landscape of a Teacher's Life*, San Francisco, Jossey-Bass.

Pannenberg, Wolfhart, 1998. *Systematic Theology*, vol. 3, Edinburgh, T. & T. Clark.

Park, Tarjei, 1998. *The English Mystics: An Anthology*, London, SPCK.

Patterson, Sue, 1999. *Realist Christian Theology in a Postmodern Age*, Cambridge, Cambridge University Press.

Pedler, Mike, Burgoyne, John and Boydell, Tom, 1997. *The Learning Company: A Strategy for Sustainable Development*, London, McGraw-Hill, 2nd edn.

Perls, Frederick, Hefferline, Ralph F. and Goodman, Paul, 1996. *Gestalt Therapy: Excitement and Growth in the Human Personality*, London, Souvenir Press.

Polkinghorne, John, 1990. *The Quantum World*, London, Penguin.

Reininger, Gustave (ed.), 1999. *The Diversity of Centring Prayer*, New York, Continuum.

Roman Catholic Bishops' report, 1995. *The Sign We Give*, Roman Catholic Bishops' Conference of England and Wales.

Scheler, Max, 1996, in J. G. Williams, 1996.

Schillebeeckx, Edward, 1980. 'A Creative Retrospect as Inspiration for the Ministry in the Future', in L. Grollenberg *et al.*, *Minister? Pastor? Prophet?* London, SCM.

Schillebeeckx, Edward, 1989. *Church: The Human Story of God*, London, SCM.

Sharpe, Kevin, 2000. *Sleuthing the Divine: The Nexus of Science and Spirit*, Minneapolis, Fortress Press.

Southcott, Ernest, 1966. *The Parish Comes Alive*, London, Mowbray.

Stapp, Henry, 1979, in G. Zukav, 1979.

Swieringa, J. and Wiersema, A., 1992, *Becoming a Learning Organisation*, Wokingham, Addison-Wesley.

Tanner, Kathryn, 1997. *Theories of Culture: A New Agenda for Theology*, Minneapolis, Fortress Press.

Thurian, Max (ed.), 1983. *Ecumenical Perspectives on Baptism, Eucharist and Ministry*, Faith and Order Paper 116, Geneva, WCC.

Torrance, Alan J., 1996. *Persons in Communion: Trinitarian Description and Human Participation*, Edinburgh, T. & T. Clark.

Vanier, Jean, 1999. *Becoming Human*, London, Darton, Longman & Todd.

Volf, Miroslav, 1998. *After Our Likeness: The Church as the Image of the Trinity*, Cambridge, Eerdmans.

Walker, Joanna, 2000/2001. 'Adult Learning and Transformation', *Ministry*, the journal of the Edward King Institute for Ministerial Development, Gloucester Diocesan Local Ministry Office, Winter.

Watson, Natalie K., 2001. 'Reconsidering Ecclesiology: Feminist Perspectives', *Theology and Sexuality*, the journal of the Centre for the Study of Christianity and Sexuality, no. 14, March.

Wheatley, Margaret, J., 1999. *Leadership and the New Science: Discovering Order in a Chaotic World*, San Francisco, Berrett-Koehler, 2nd edn.

Wilkinson, Alan, 1996. *The Church of England and the First World War*, London, SCM.

Williams, James G., 1996. *The Girard Reader*, New York, Crossroad Herder.

Winfield, Flora, 2000. *Releasing Energy: How Methodists and Anglicans Can Grow Together*, London, Church House Publishing.

Woodward, James and Pattison, Stephen, 2000. *The Blackwell Reader in Pastoral and Practical Theology*, Oxford, Blackwell.

Yong-Bock, Kim, 2000, in D. Fergusson and M. Sarot (eds), 2000.

Yontef, Gary M., 1993. *Awareness, Dialogue and Process: Essays on Gestalt Therapy*, New York, Gestalt Journal Press.

Zabriskie, Stewart C., 1995. *Total Ministry*, New York, Alban Institute.

Zizioulas, John, 1985. *Being as Communion*, London, Darton, Longman & Todd.

Zukav, Gary, 1979. *The Dancing Wu Li Masters: An Overview of the New Physics*, New York, Quill, William Morrow.

Index